MAS'
YOUR
PSYCHIC
POWERS

MASTER YOUR PSYCHIC POWERS

How to Gain Greater Control of Your Life

BILLY ROBERTS

BLANDFORD

A BLANDFORD BOOK
First published in the UK 1998 by Blandford
a Cassell Imprint

Cassell & Co.,
Wellington House,125 Strand
London WC2R OBB

Distributed in the United States by Sterling Publishing Co., Inc.
387 Park Avenue South, New York, NY 10016-8810

A Cataloguing-in-Publication Data entry for this title
is available from the British Library

ISBN 0-7137-2716-0

Designed by Richard Carr
Cover design by Jamie Tanner
Printed and bound in Great Britain by MPG Books Ltd,
Bodmin, Cornwall

Contents

INTRODUCTION

*I*N THESE LIBERATED times we no longer feel the need to glance anxiously over our shoulder before whispering the old taboo words such as 'paranormal', 'psychic' or 'supernatural'. Today, these words raise few eyebrows – quite the contrary in fact, as a quick check through any weekly television listings will show. You will doubtless spot more than a couple of programmes concerned, in one way or another, with psychic and supernatural matters. A certain sort of, dare I say, 'credibility' seems currently to be hovering around the edges of the paranormal.

So, just what *are* our psychic abilities, and why should we strive to develop them? What, if anything, is in it for us?

These psychic powers about which we hear so much these days are, broadly speaking, those abilities we possess for which today's science has no explanation. Clairvoyance, healing, precognition, telepathy, mediumship, are all examples of psychic abilities. By developing your psychic powers you will gain much greater control of your own life. You will find yourself becoming more assertive and positive in both outlook and approach. Your psychic self will help you to achieve your aims and reach your goals.

Prior to the development of even the most rudimentary form of language, it is believed that primitive man communicated his thoughts and feelings telepathically. I remember reading somewhere that speech was only evolved to enable man to lie.

Whether or not this indictment is true, of one thing we can rest assured, and that is that modern man has certainly forgotten, if not lost completely, most of the psychic abilities possessed by his primitive brothers. The reason for this loss is simple. Modern man, living as he does today, would have little use for his ancestors' psychic abilities. How would they fit into this age of science, technology and 'reason'?

Psychic development today is, therefore, not so much a case of receiving knowledge as it is of remembering. With this in mind, it is not my intention in this book to teach you anything; I will merely try to remind you of what you have long since forgotten.

From my own experience, I know only too well just how difficult it is to choose something suitable from the many books displayed on the shelves in bookshops today. So many of them offer a variety of quick and easy methods for developing your own psychic abilities. How do you pick the one that is right for you? This can often dishearten the most sincere 'student' of psychic development who, finding it all too confusing, may therefore decide to pursue the subject no further.

Having myself encountered many of the problems and pitfalls which pave the road of psychic development, I have put together a few ideas and designed a series of programmes which I feel may be of some help to you as you move towards the development and expansion of your psychic self.

Remember the ancient precept: 'When the student is ready the teacher will always appear.' This is as right and meaningful today as it was when it was first written. For, in my experience, when the time is right an opportunity will always present itself. This opportunity may be anything from a chance meeting with a knowledgeable teacher, to a book whose title almost jumps out at you from its place on a shelf in your local bookstore.

However, there are no short routes where psychic development is concerned, no corners which can be cut. Your endeavour to develop the psychic faculties may, in fact, be an extremely difficult and at times painful task, during which one needs to be keenly vigilant, extremely patient and certainly self-critical.

Always beware of praise and flattery, for whether or not it is honestly given, it can lull you into a false sense of security, causing complacency and vanity, both of which are extremely self-destructive where the science of psychic development is concerned.

I have found psychic development to be an extremely solitary and even lonely path to follow. Its call for total dedication can disrupt one's social life. On the other hand it does have its rewards, not the least of which is the development of a fuller and more complete awareness of the world in which one lives, and a greater realization of the soul and its independence of the physical body.

I have never believed that it is enough to merely develop the psychic faculties, in isolation so to speak, while having little or no knowledge of their background and mechanics, i.e. of what they are, how they work and where they come from. One would not expect a surgeon to perform delicate and complicated operations without any prior knowledge of the physiological and anatomical make-up of man.

I am often reminded of the profound words of the mystic and dramatist Maurice Maeterlinck:

> *The wise man is not he who sees, but he who seeing furthest, has the greatest love and understanding for all mankind. He who sees without loving and understanding is only straining his eyes in the darkness.*

Maeterlinck's words speak volumes, I feel. It is with their sentiment in mind that I have included here, in Chapter 1, an outline of man's subtle anatomy, the aura, and the mechanics of psychic development. Over the years I have made a study of various methods and techniques of meditation, and of exercises for quietening the mind. From these I have designed a programme of meditation which is extremely effective in the precipitation of psychic awareness. This is also included in the text. Readers should first read the book through, then select that which is appropriate and which will work most effectively for them. One of the main obstacles one faces when endeavouring to develop one's psychic abilities is the doubt that it can ever be achieved. Thus it is important to realize that everyone possesses psychic powers potentially, and it is wrong to surmise that a psychic ability which is not immediately apparent cannot be developed and cultivated.

Of course, some people do have greater potential than others, and may, therefore, develop their psychic skills in a shorter period of time. None the less, the potential to develop psychic powers lies within each and every one of us, and can most certainly be encouraged and developed by the use of specific techniques.

It is also wrong to assume that a psychic ability which one already possesses cannot in any way be further refined and developed. A psychic power is like any other mental power – it most certainly can be improved upon and developed to its fullest potential.

HOW PSYCHIC ARE YOU?

1. Do you ever sense that the telephone is going to ring, and it does?

2. Do you sometimes know what your partner is going to say just before they speak?

3. Do you ever have strong feelings about something that is going to happen, and it does?

4. Have you ever been alone in the house and suddenly felt as though someone is watching you, or standing behind you?

5. Have you ever felt uncomfortable while sitting alone in a theatre or waiting in a bus queue, and when you looked over your shoulder someone was staring at you?

6. Do you ever dream about specific things or situations which later happen?

7. Do you ever see pinpoints of bright light around people's heads, or pinpoints of colour floating in the air?

8. Have you ever seen a coloured mist around people or animals?

9. Have you ever thought you have seen a shadowy figure out of the corner of your eye while you were alone in the house?

10. Have you ever met someone for the first time and felt certain that you know them from somewhere, although you don't?

11. Have you ever walked into a house for the first time and immediately been overwhelmed by its warmth; coldness; happiness; sadness?

12. When you are drifting into sleep do you ever hear someone call your name?

13. Have you ever been overwhelmed by a fragrance that no one else can smell, and which reminds you of a dead relative or friend?

14. Have you ever handled a piece of antique jewellery and found pictures and impressions forming in your mind?

15. Have strong feelings ever forewarned you not to go to a certain place or do a particular thing?

16. Have you ever had bad feelings about someone whom everyone else likes?

17. When someone is unwell do you ever feel compelled to place your hands on them in an attempt to make them better?

18. Have you ever seen the patterns on curtains or carpets change into faces?

19. Have you ever been overwhelmed with the feeling that a relative or friend, living on the other side of the world, has had an accident, and you later learned that they had?

20. Have you ever felt compelled to write a poem or a piece of philosophical writing which, on later examination, appears completely alien to the way you think?

It is quite common to have experienced two or perhaps three of the things listed above. However, to have experienced six or seven of them shows that you have psychic potential. If you can answer 'yes' to ten, or even all the things listed, you most certainly do have a psychic ability. Read on.

chapter 1

THE AURA

*I*F YOU WANT to be trendy and New Age these days, all you have to do is talk about the aura as if it were an old friend. Unfortunately, the aura's new-found popularity has led it to become a greatly misunderstood aspect of man's subtle anatomy. Obviously, the word 'aura' is often used without any understanding of its true meaning. We have all heard, for example, the expressions 'He has an aura of serenity about him', or 'The house has an aura of happiness and warmth'.

In fact, the word AURA suggests the existence of a subtle atmosphere emanating from, and surrounding, all living things.

WHAT IS THE AURA?

I suppose the aura is best and most simply described as a vaporous mass of electromagnetic particles surrounding both animate and inanimate matter. It is, in fact, an energy field. However, the aura which emanates from the human form differs in more ways than one from that which emanates from an inanimate object, for the human aura represents the degree (level) of life and consciousness present. Although the presence of consciousness and life in both animate and inanimate matter is measured merely in degrees (levels), the aura which emanates from animate matter is completely different in both appearance and movement from the aura which emanates from inanimate matter, even though life is still present in the inanimate state, albeit at a lower level.

In comparison to the aura of an inanimate object, the human energy field is a veritable kaleidoscope of colours, and is full of movement as it radiates outward from the body. In the human aura the degree or level of vitality present in the body is exhibited in the aura in the consistency of radiation lines, and the combinations and frequency of colours, their shades and strengths.

The human aura is in fact more luminous than the inanimate aura, and changes with the person's every passing thought, feeling and impulse of emotion. Therefore, the one who is able to perceive the human energy field in its totality (and not just one or two aspects of it) is able to gain access to an abundance of personal information about the person from whom the aura emanates. From the aura, the one who possesses 'vision' (and this is, of course, a psychic skill) can determine a person's state of mental, emotional and physical health. The spiritual progress which a person has attained will be evident, from the aura as a whole, to the one who 'sees'. It therefore makes sense that as long as what is seen in the aura is interpreted correctly, a person's true character will be revealed. And I do mean the *true* character because, to the one who possesses 'vision', the truth will always be clearly visible behind the façade of falsehood.

The aura has been discussed and depicted in many ways over thousands of years in religious, cultural and artistic circles. An obvious example is the head-dress of a North American Indian chief, which symbolizes the aura and its many colours. The beautiful display of colour in the head-dress represents the wearer's wisdom and status in his tribe – the greater the variety of colour, the higher his level of spirituality.

The halo, traditionally painted around or over the heads of saints by medieval artists, also represented an aspect of the aura, depicting the exalted state, or divinity, of the individual. The very fact that the artists painted the halo at all shows us that they must have been aware of the aura's existence, even though the subtle glow of golden light which they painted around the head is a mere part of what there actually is to be seen in the whole. For the aura, when seen in its entirety, obscures the whole body with colour and movement, emanating outward from it into the surrounding space.

The tonsure of the monk (shaven head) was not just some aberration which caught on among those God-fearing folk, but was done in order to fully expose both the crown chakra (*Sahasrara*), and the aura around the head, to God and cosmic influences.

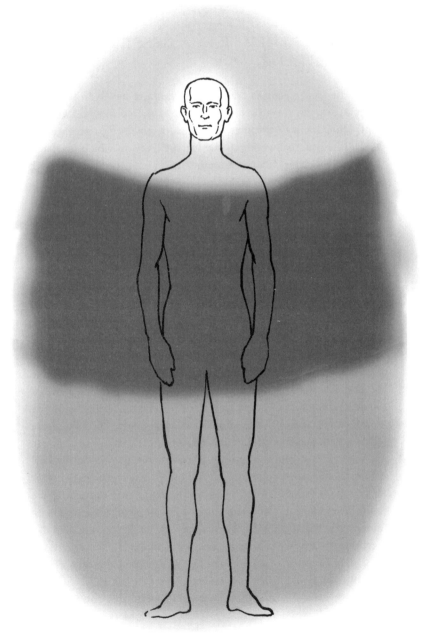

The aura of a well-balanced, sensitive thinker, with an intellectual mind. The human aura can be described as a luminous, colourful energy field surrounding each individual. Learning to work with the aura is fundamental to developing any psychic potential.

HOW DOES THE AURA MANIFEST, AND WHAT TRANSMITS IT?

Before the soul becomes embodied in flesh, it travels in vibratory descent through the manifested worlds of the cosmos, drawing to itself along its way sheaves or bodies of energy. These sheaves enable the soul to function at the various levels to which it relates, and through which it descends, before it eventually becomes encased, so to speak, in a physical body.

To enable the soul to exist in, and compete with, the alien circumstances in which it finds itself when encased in a physical body, it is necessary for it to be cosmically sustained, not only at a physical level, but also at the various other levels to which each of its other bodies relate. This need for cosmic sustenance necessitates the formation of a system of 'psychic energy points' whose vital job it is to control and correct the in-pouring cosmic energy. These psychic energy points perform the function of small, subtle transformers, modifying, transmuting and distributing the energy coming into the body (rather like electrical transformers stepping down a current of electricity) and thus maintaining man's equilibrium at all levels. These 'psychic transformers' are called 'chakras', which in Sanskrit means 'wheels' or 'circles', and they play an extremely important part in the development and evolution of man's consciousness. The role of the chakras will be discussed fully in Chapter 2.

We know, of course, that man is much more than just a physical frame. In fact, man's subtle anatomy consists of seven vehicles or bodies of energy, which, while of necessity restricting and preventing the soul's full expression, also enable man's consciousness to manifest upon the seven corresponding planes. Each of these bodies is composed of a much finer material than the one below it, and they rise, in a gradually ascending vibratory scale, from the lowest, densest and most apparent (the physical body), to the highest and purest (the spirit).

The following analogy may help to illustrate this concept more fully. Consider for a few moments that you are observing a container of molten wax being poured into a bowl of cold water. On entering the water the molten wax slowly solidifies to enable it to compete with the alien circumstances (the water) in which it finds itself. The liquid wax gradually solidifies, layer upon layer, rather like the soul which, on its downward vibratory journey through the supersensual universe, will eventually become embodied in flesh.

Although this is a very simple analogy, it is, I feel, one that illustrates the concept perfectly well. For the soul, too, lives in an alien environment during its sojourn in this physical world. However, while it dwells here the soul, and its various subtle bodies of expression, need to be energized. The energy created by and radiating from *all* of man's subtle bodies combined is what constitutes the aura, and this beautiful, kaleidoscopic, vaporous mass, thus formed, is what sets man apart from all other living things.

HOW DO WE KNOW THE AURA EXISTS?

Modern technology has advanced to such an extent in this area that the aura can now actually be photographed in colour. The photographic technique presently employed in order to obtain these fascinating photographs is far superior to that initially developed by Semyon and Valentina Kirlian, a husband-and-wife team from Krasnodar near the Black Sea. They were the first people to photograph the aura. Some years ago 'screens' were developed, containing a special dye, which enabled the user, when looking through them, to 'see' the auric field. These screens were developed by Dr Walter Kilner, a radiologist at St Thomas's Hospital, London. Dr Kilner's extensive study of the human aura led him to write a book about it entitled *The Human Atmosphere*. This book was, in fact, an inspiration to others working in the same field, and it gave rise to further research on the aura. Kilner was reputed to be the first man to scientifically observe the aura and, as a result of his studies, many diseases can now be diagnosed and thus treated through the aura.

The aura certainly does not have to be seen for its existence to be felt. On the contrary, many people who work with the aura, in particular those working in the field of healing, develop a natural sensitivity to it. It is probably true to say that most healers can 'sense' the aura, and, through their ability to 'sense', will often find their hands drawn to the affected part of the body they are seeking to treat. This may be because the healer feels intense heat, or perhaps coldness, around the troubled area, telling him or her instinctively that he or she has located the spot at which treatment is needed.

However, whether or not you are a healer is immaterial, for sensing the aura is a phenomenon that most people have experienced in one way or another, at some time in their lives, whether they know it or not. For example, you may be sitting in a theatre, or perhaps standing in a bus queue, when an uncomfortable, nagging feeling makes you turn round. On so doing, you catch the eye of someone who is staring intently at you. You can certainly 'feel' the person's eyes almost burning a hole in the back of your head – that is why you turned round. Or you may perhaps have been alone in the house at some time, occupied with the housework, your attention on the cleaning or tidying. You suddenly become convinced that someone is standing behind you, and you turn round quickly. Yet there is no one there, and the house remains quiet and empty. Or, again when you have been alone somewhere, either at home or in the office, you may suddenly have experienced an overwhelming smell of perfume or aftershave which unexpectedly washes over your senses, reminding you of a dead relative or friend. All these phenomena are experienced through the medium of the aura.

HOW IS THIS POSSIBLE? WHAT SUBTLE ENERGY IS AT WORK?

In my studies of the aura I have found it to be more sensitive at a person's back, and in fact proportionately larger there, extending further out from the body, than at the front. However, this does not seem to be the case with a blind person, where the aura tends to be equal in the distance it extends outwards all around the body. The absence of sight causes the aura at the front to be more developed than is the case with a sighted person. This extra development takes place in order to compensate for the absence of vision, and usually allows the sensitivity and awareness of the visually handicapped person to be heightened. In other words, the aura is our 'antenna' and, surrounding us completely, is constantly working to protect us from harm. In a crowded theatre, for example, the aura usually contracts, forming a sort of protective shell around the person. However, once that person feels relaxed and more comfortable sitting among strangers, the aura gradually expands to blend and thus merge with

the collective aurae of the rest of the audience. The collective energy field of a crowd is quite a sight to behold. The beautiful display of colour constantly moves and changes, revealing, of course, the changing moods and thought patterns of the people present.

HOW CAN ONE DEVELOP THE ABILITY TO 'SEE' THE AURA?

It is important to understand that nearly all psychic phenomena experienced by man manifest, in one way or another, through the medium of the aura.

Learning to work with the aura is very important when endeavouring to develop any psychic potential. Once you have mastered the ability to control and expand your own aura, you will very quickly realize just what power you have within you. The more you develop your auric abilities, the greater the control you will have over your own life and the environment in which you live. Whether you 'see' or merely 'sense' the aura, this skill will enable you to 'read' others like an open book. The stronger your ability becomes, the more powerfully accurate your powers will be.

The ability to see the aura can most certainly be developed. However, before any attempt is made to do so, it would be a good idea first to find out exactly what the aura looks like; then you will know what it is you are looking for, and will, therefore, be able to identify 'it' when you see it.

Most, if not all people, have seen an aspect of the aura at some time or other, even though they may have been completely unaware of it at the time. This is usually because, when the experience occurs, it is often dismissed as either a trick of the light, or perhaps put down to tired eyes. For example, you may, on occasion, have been so engrossed in conversation with a friend that time has flown by, and you have failed to notice the sunlight fading and casting shadows across the room. Eventually your attention wanders for a moment, and at that point you may see a pale band of light around your friend's head. Of course, when you move your eyes to focus on it directly, it disappears. Out of the corner of your eye you may have seen a similar band of light around a chair, or even round a picture hanging on the wall. In fact, you would be forgiven for dismissing this phenomenon as a trick of the light, or the result of your tired eyes. After all, listening intently to what your friend has been saying will cause the optic lens to become fatigued. The subdued lighting, and the effort of your concentration, will put everything out of focus, causing the eyes to see things almost out of perspective. Difficult as it may be to believe, that pale band of light which you saw around your friend's head is actually an aspect of the aura. It became visible to you because your eyes were tired, and because of the subdued lighting.

One of the techniques used for developing the ability to 'see' the aura is, in fact, the age-old art of 'scrying'. Scrying has come to mean crystal gazing, although traditionally it is the ancient art of staring at any focal point. The focal point can be anything from a crystal ball to the flame of a lighted candle, or even a piece of quartz crystal placed in front of a lighted candle. Personally I would recommend the lighted candle technique, as I have always found it to be the most effective.

Exercise 1

All you need is a comfortable chair and a lighted candle. It sometimes helps the concentration if you burn some incense and play some quiet, meditative music in the background. Light your candle and place it on a surface in front of you, as near to eye level as possible. Either lower the lights or turn them out completely, whichever you prefer. Settle yourself comfortably in the chair, making sure that your chest, neck and head are as nearly in a straight line as possible. Pull your shoulders slightly back, and rest your hands lightly in your lap.

Move your gaze slowly to the tip of the candle's flame and stare at it. Try not to blink or to move your eyes away from the flame, even for a moment. To aid your concentration and help you to relax, begin to breathe deeply and slowly, allowing your stomach to rise as you breathe in, to fall as you breathe out, and so on.

When you feel that you can no longer gaze at the flame without blinking (your eyes will become 'gritty' and you will feel the need to blink to clear them), close your eyes very slowly. As you do so, place the palms of your hands over them. Within a few moments the after image of the flame will gradually appear in your mind's eye.

The object of this exercise is to hold the image of the flame in your mind's eye for as long as you possibly can. Holding it steady in your mind, continue to breathe in a slow and easy rhythm. You will begin to notice that with each inhalation the image of the flame will grow stronger and more clearly defined. However, when the after image eventually becomes fragmented and begins to fade, open your eyes, and very slowly return your gaze to the flame. Repeat the process.

At first the exercise should be repeated only three or four times in one sitting, but when you feel comfortable with it, the number of times should be increased to six or seven. In time, with practice and determination, you should find that the after image of the flame will remain easily in the mind's eye, and will not fade until you allow it to do so.

The benefits of this exercise can be quite startling. Not only does regular practice help to improve the concentration and cultivate one's ability to visualize, but your powers of observation will also improve Practised over long periods of time, this exercise will stimulate the psychic visual response mechanism, precipitating the ability to 'see clearly'. It certainly cultivates any latent clairvoyant abilities the practitioner may have, and makes one more visually sensitive to auric emanations. One cautionary note however: it is advisable to remove contact lenses, if worn, before using this technique.

Once the aura becomes visible to you it is essential to maintain a positive attitude when interpreting what is seen. For seeing the aura opens up a whole new and extremely exciting aspect to the supersensual universe. In fact, seeing it is only the beginning, as the interpretation of the colours, their numerous shades, degrees and combinations varies widely among those who see, or who claim to see, the aura in its entirety. However, it is not my intention in this book to become embroiled in the debate over the interpretation of auric colours. In my opinion this is very much a case of 'whatever works for you', and only practice and experience will help you along the way.

 ## Exercise 2

Slice a fresh, red apple into four pieces and remove the dark brown pips. The pips must be dark brown, as opposed to white, as the dark colour is crucial to this experiment.

Place the pips on a piece of white paper and stare at them for a few moments. Try not to let your gaze wander. In a very short time you will begin to see a faint glow around the outline of the pips – a sort of pale blue vapour, which will seem to move around the pips in a clockwise motion. The longer you stare at the pips the stronger the vaporous glow around them will become.

What you are actually seeing is the aura of the pips, i.e. the energy radiating from them. As you continue to watch the aura moving around the pips, you will notice fine streams of energy emanating from them. These streams of energy represent the vitality present in the pips, and their general health. If you move the pips about an inch apart, you will see the energy radiating from one of them actually reach out to the other, until it blends with it. The pips will appear to be totally in phase with each other.

For the next part of the experiment place these same pips in an envelope and put them away for 24 hours. Then remove them from the envelope and again place them on a piece of white paper, alongside some fresh pips just taken from another apple.

You will notice that the vaporous glow around the old pips will not now appear quite as bright and vibrant, in comparison to the energy radiating from the fresh pips. The streams of energy that were apparent when the pips were fresh will now appear to be slowly fading, in rather the same way as the energy which can be seen radiating from a sick or dying person. However, wait a few moments and something quite remarkable will begin to happen. You will see the energy radiating from the fresh pips begin to reach out to the dry pips in a desperate effort to revitalize them. For a while the older pips may appear to recover, but this recovery is not permanent, and eventually they will wither and die.

The object of this experiment is not only to let you see exactly what the aura looks like, but also to show you just how a healthy aura, full of vitality, can positively affect an unhealthy one lacking such vitality. This process of 'passing on' energy should be of great interest to those endeavouring to develop the ability to heal. Although strictly speaking, this book is not concerned with the development of healing skills I will be covering the concept of *energy*, and how it is used during psychic development, in Chapter 3. I have included some useful tips on how best to control this energy, something which should be extremely beneficial to any aspiring healer.

As I have mentioned above, most if not all psychic abilities manifest in one way or another through the medium of the aura, and it is through the aura that subtle vibrations are transmitted and received.

How many times have you been thinking about someone from

whom you haven't heard for a while and, only a short time later, they telephone you, or even knock on your door? This might, of course, be put down to coincidence or chance but, more often than not, it is the result of telepathy, or mind-to-mind communication.

If we work on the premise that 'thoughts are living things', then it certainly makes sense to accept that those thoughts are capable of being projected, either consciously or otherwise, almost instantaneously, from one place to another, unrestricted by time or space. In fact, a small experiment can easily prove this

 ## Exercise 3

Ask a friend to sit quietly in another room, with a pencil and paper to hand. Tell them to close their eyes and wait until they feel inspired to draw something.

Sit quietly by yourself, your eyes closed. Think of a shape, a word or an object. Build up whatever you have chosen very clearly in your mind, and then slowly transmit it to your friend in the adjacent room.

The most effective method of transmitting pictures is to precede the transmission with some gentle, slow, rhythmic breathing, projecting your picture on each exhalation. In this way you give the telepathic process a rhythmic flow, which is important to effect positive telepathic results. Do not be disappointed if the experiment proves unsuccessful at first. On occasion, a rapport with your 'partner' has to be created before clear mental images can be successfully transmitted and received. Although telepathic communication can sometimes be quite spontaneous, the ability usually needs to be worked at and developed. Of course, as is the case with everything, practice and determination always bring about positive, successful results. Once the telepathic flow has been successfully achieved the 'receiver' will see the pictures very clearly in their mind, just as in our first exercise, you 'saw' the flame of a candle.

A frequent mistake is for the 'receiver' to question the pictures which they see floating through their consciousness.

Try not to stop, think and question, as this will interfere with any successful transmission. It is important to respond immediately to the impressions which float into the mind by drawing them, and thus acknowledging receipt.

As with all psychic impressions, telepathic images can be fleeting, and will be strengthened only through an immediate response. Once psychic images have been successfully transmitted and received, the 'transmitter' should have a turn at receiving. Only when seven or more transmissions have been successfully received consistently, over a period of a week or more, can one safely regard the telepathic exercise as successful.

I mentioned earlier the importance of learning to work with the aura. To this end you will find the following exercise invaluable.

 ## Exercise 4a

The ability to expand and contract your aura is an ability which, in fact, comes quite naturally to everyone.

You will need to work with a partner. Choose someone with whom you feel comfortable. You will also need a pair of divining rods. Should you not be able to obtain these, they are quite simple to make. Cut two lengths of wire, approximately 15–18in. (38–46cm.) in length, from two wire coat hangers. Bend each piece into an 'L' shape. Take one wire rod in each hand and, gripping them loosely by the short length, point them in front of you. When the divining rods locate a source of energy, they will either cross over each other or turn away from each other.

Ask your partner to hide an object, tell your divining rods to locate the hidden object – and see what happens.

Hold the rods in front of you and allow them to lead you. Try to be aware of any sensations you feel in your hands. You may experience tingling or even some vibration.

It may take some time to familiarize yourself with your divining rods, but with patience and practice results will be achieved.

 ## Exercise 4b

Ask your partner to stand with their back against a wall. Stand facing them at a distance of at least 6ft. (approx. 182 cm.). Holding the divining rods in front of you, pointing towards your partner, walk slowly towards them until the rods either cross over or move apart. This point, the point at which the rods move, is where your partner's aura begins.

Repeat the exercise, but this time ask your partner to stand facing the wall. Again from some distance, begin to approach them slowly, stopping when the rods begin to move. This time you should notice that the point at which the rods begin to move will be considerably further away from your partner, showing that the aura at the rear is proportionately greater, extending further out from the body, than at the front.

Change places and ask your partner to 'home in' on you with the divining rods. Compare the difference in aura sizes.

 ## Exercise 4c

Ask your friend to repeat the exercise, homing in on you with the divining rods, but this time close your eyes and cover your ears to block out any sound. Before your friend moves towards you they should stand quietly for a few moments in order to create in you a feeling of anticipation. This feeling of uncertainty, and possibly apprehension, actually causes the aura to expand in anticipation of the approaching 'danger'.

This auric expansion will be apparent in the movement of the divining rods. Repeat the experiment, this time with your back to your partner, and note just how much your aura expands.

Practising this method at least twice a day will enable you to master the ability to control and project your auric energies. The benefits will enhance your everyday life, as well as your psychic work, and will certainly strengthen your personality, making you more positive in everything you do.

As one can exercise the physical body to improve its muscle tone, mind power can also be exercised to improve one's mental and psychic abilities. At the end of this book (Chapter 11), I will examine different types of meditation which are specifically designed to improve such skills, to heighten your awareness of the aura, and to infuse it with vitality. Meditation *must*, without a doubt, play an extremely important part in the development of the psychic faculties, and it must be used in your personal daily programme.

chapter 2

ACTIVATING THE CHAKRAS

AN IS AN extremely complex being, and is much more than just a physical body. He is a veritable powerhouse of energy, encased within a vibratory spectrum of numerous sheaths or bodies, each one composed of a much finer material than the one below it.

The whole of man's subtle anatomy is permeated by a complex network of etheric wiring along which energy is conveyed to the organs of the physical body, thereby maintaining man's equilibrium on all levels of consciousness. All this energy is controlled, so to speak, by a complex system of subtle energy centres which, as I have mentioned, are called 'chakras' in Sanskrit, meaning 'wheels' or 'circles'.

It is the main purpose of this chapter to explain how your psychic abilities work, and to show you that it is possible to improve those abilities simply by increasing the activity of your chakras.

The chakras appear to be connected in some way to various major glands of the physical body. They are responsible for the distribution of energy and for the development and evolution of man's consciousness. Some esoteric schools of thought believe the chakra system to be a type of memory bank, within which are stored experience data from the present and previous incarnations. They represent the various degrees of man's consciousness, and although all the chakras are potentially present at birth, only one can be seen to be fully

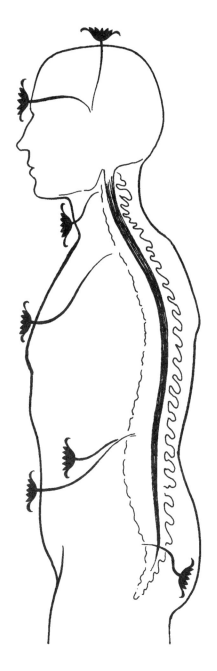

Side view of the chakras.

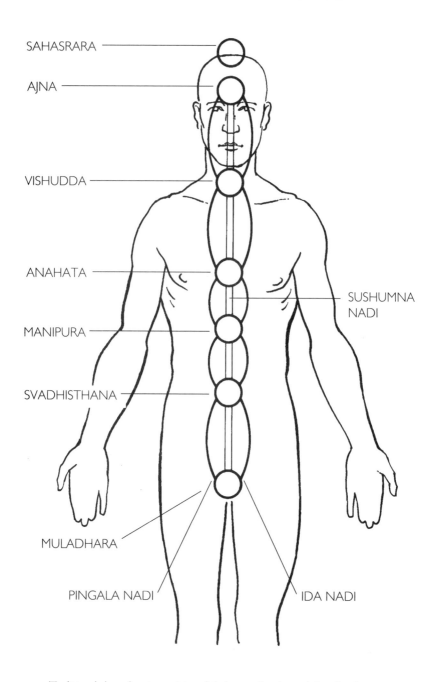

SAHASRARA

AJNA

VISHUDDA

ANAHATA

SUSHUMNA
NADI

MANIPURA

SVADHISTHANA

MULADHARA

PINGALA NADI

IDA NADI

Traditional chart showing position of chakras and nadis, and their Sanskrit names.

activated at that time. The others take a full seven-year cycle before activity in them becomes apparent, at the rate of one chakra a year.

Literally thousands of chakras permeate man's subtle anatomy. They are major and minor vortices of energy, modifying and distributing the in-coming force, and maintaining a well-balanced individual in body, mind and soul.

However, there are seven major centres which are considered primary. These are perceived as saucer-like impressions across the surface of the etheric body, having the appearance of small flowers whose petals increase in number as they ascend the spine.

The first chakra to become activated, at birth, is called 'Muladhara', and it is situated at the base of the spine. This extremely important centre limits the new-born baby's awareness to the instinctive level, and is, in fact, responsible for all its babyish actions, from crying to be fed, to reaching instinctively for its mother's breast.

Thus, the chakras open in sequence, at the rate of one a year, beginning with the centre at the base of the spine, and concluding the chakric cycle (when the child is 7 years old) with the centre on the crown of the head called 'Sahasrara'.

As the child continues to grow through the first seven-year cycle of life, energy is transferred from one chakra to the other, causing each one to be vivified, and to coruscate with kaleidoscopic whirlpools of colour. Some chakras may become more active than others and this will cause the child's awareness at that level to be influenced, often precipitating a latent ability such as an aptitude for the creative arts, i.e. music, painting, or perhaps creative writing.

Even the child who dreams about being a doctor, and who shows a propensity for medical knowledge at an early age, is influenced by the appropriate chakra, and will most certainly achieve his or her dream when he or she grows up. Such qualities in a child do not come about by chance or coincidence. Sometimes there is such a powerful force within a specific chakra that the child can be so strongly influenced as to appear far in advance of his or her years; hence the child prodigies about whom we hear from time to time.

The child who is extremely sensitive and caring, always wanting to look after people, is strongly influenced by the chakra situated in the area of the heart called 'Anahata'. This is the centre that appears to influence a person's emotional sensitivity, and controls the life of someone dedicated to a caring profession, such as a nurse or a doctor or, in the psychic field, a healer.

The person who is good at his or her job, and enjoys doing it, is strongly influenced by the chakras corresponding to their ability. For example, the person who has been trained to listen and to give advice, and who is, in fact, extremely good at what he or she does, is influenced by the chakras situated in the throat and between the eyebrows.

The chakra in the throat area is called 'Vishudda' and when active it influences the auditory faculties. *Vishudda* is also responsible for the psychic ability known as 'clairaudience' – the gift of 'hearing' the voices of the so-called 'dead'.

The chakra between the eye brows is called '*Ajna*' and is responsible for the ability to 'see'. Anyone who is extremely observant and notices detail is influenced by this chakra. This centre is situated in the seat of the traditional 'third eye', and is responsible for the psychic ability known as 'clairvoyance'.

It is important to note, however, that a psychic ability such as clairvoyance or clairaudience will only manifest through the appropriate chakra when the second and third chakras have also been activated. These chakras, '*Svadisthana*' and '*Manipura*', together form a vital part of man's subtle anatomy. *Manipura* is associated with the solar plexus, or, in yogic parlance, 'the sun centre', and is the powerhouse of all of man's psychic abilities.

Everything said thus far will probably be academic, so, to enable you to see that the chakras *do* exist, I would like you to experience them for yourself. With the help of a few simple experiments you can become more aware of the chakras, and will be able to use them to your advantage.

 Exercise 5

For the experiment you will need to work with a partner.

Stand up straight, with your left hand by your side and your right arm extended in front of you. Allow your partner (using one hand) to gently push your arm down, but resist

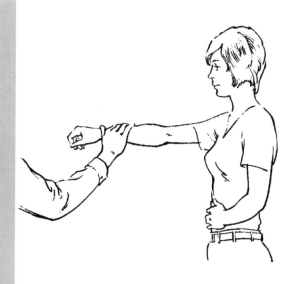

their pressure just enough to make clear how much strength you possess in your arm. You will need to know this for purposes of comparison later. Having done this, rest your arm for a moment.

Repeat the process. However, this time, while your partner is applying pressure to your right arm, place your left hand over the area of *Muladhara* (the genital area). Make a note of any changes in the strength of your right arm. Rest your arm.

Repeat the process. This time, place your left hand gently over the area of *Svadisthana* (your naval). Again, make a note of any changes to the strength of your right arm. Rest your arm.

Repeat the process. Move your left hand to the area of *Manipura*, immediately below the left-hand side of the rib cage, slightly above the naval. Make a note of any changes in the strength of your right arm, as your partner applies a little pressure to it. Rest your arm.

Repeat the process, working your way through all seven chakras, from the base chakra to the crown, noting their condition as you go.

INTERPRETING YOUR RESULTS

This simple experiment allows you to note the condition of each chakra. If your arm feels weak when your hand is placed over the area of the first chakra (*Muladhara*) this will mean that little activity is present at that point. It will therefore indicate that you are perhaps currently a little run down. However, should your right arm exhibit an increase of strength, this would be indicative of someone with a great deal of vitality and stamina.

Should the second and third chakras show signs of weakness or underactivity (*Svadisthana* and *Manipura*), this would indicate that you are a nervy person, perhaps a little too sensitive or lacking in confidence. However, if they exhibit a surge of strength, this will reveal your inner strength and confidence, and your ability to cope in times of stress and crisis. The fourth chakra (*Anahata*) reveals the balance of your life. Should it show signs of weakness or inactivity, this would show emotional insecurity, sadness, and lack of confidence. However, should *Anahata* prove to be strong when pressure is applied to your right arm, this would reveal stability, warmth, compassion and control of the emotions.

If weakness is exhibited in the throat area or fifth chakra (*Vishudda*), this would indicate that you are sluggish, slow to respond, do not pay attention and find it difficult to concentrate for any length of time. However, should strength be found in that area, you are probably versatile, resourceful, creative and observant. It would also mean that psychic abilities are inherent, and that this psychic centre is open to the supersensual impulses of the psychic world. Should the sixth chakra (*Ajna*) appear weak when pressure is applied to your extended right arm, you lack the ability to concentrate, and you probably do not overtax your imagination. You probably lack imagination and drive, and have no real ambition or deep interest in anything in particular. You may also suffer from frequent headaches, due to an insufficient flow of energy into that chakra. However, should *Ajna* appear strong, you are observant, you notice detail, your senses are very sharp and you most certainly possess potential psychic abilities. While *Sahasrara*, the crown chakra, is largely neutral in all people, its very existence links man to God and the cosmos, determining his spiritual status. This chakra plays an important role in man's spiritual evolution, so it cannot, therefore, be influenced.

ACTIVATING THE CHAKRAS

Activating the chakras and infusing them with more energy can make you more psychic. There are various methods that may be considered useful for the activation of the chakras. One is a specific technique of meditation which I shall discuss in Chapter 8. However, the simplest method of chakra activation, and one which requires no great effort on your part, is, in my opinion, one of the most effective.

 Exercise 6

Not only does this exercise infuse the chakras with vitality and power, but there is often a feeling of general wellbeing as a result. It has the effect of almost washing one's aura with a powerful surge of energy, thus heightening one's general awareness.

You will need a piece of amethyst crystal and a piece of clear quartz crystal, both small enough to hold comfortably in your hands. Amethyst, the spiritual stone, possesses calming qualities that affect the emotions and nervous system. It also heightens spiritual awareness. Clear quartz is an energy enhancer, increasing the energy in anything placed close to it. It has the effect of clearing the mind and sharpening the senses.

Sitting comfortably with your back straight, take the piece of amethyst in your right hand and the clear quartz in your left, and sit quietly with your eyes closed and both hands in your lap.

Remain in this position until the mind has become quiet. Place your right hand, holding the piece of amethyst, gently on top of your head. Place your left hand, holding the piece of clear quartz, at the base of your spine.

Remain in this position until you feel the temperature change in your right hand on top of your head. At this point swap your hands around, and place your left hand (with the quartz) on top of your head, and your right hand (with the amethyst) at the base of your spine.

Repeat the process.

Continue to repeat the exercise until both hands have rested on the head at least ten times. Then sit quietly for a further ten minutes with your eyes closed, allowing the energy to circulate around your body. If you have practised the exercise correctly you may feel your spine, forehead and hands tingling. You may also experience a feeling of disorientation as though you have breathed in fresh mountain air.

There are many benefits to be gained from this 'infusing' method. It is also effective in promoting calmness and serenity, and in easing pain.

Twenty minutes after you have completed this exercise repeat Exercise 5. Make a note of any significant changes in the results. If you can see a marked improvement in your inactive chakras there will be little need for you to use any other method of chakra activation, unless of course you do not feel comfortable with this particular one.

 # Exercise 7

Sit in a comfortable chair for five or ten minutes, until the mind becomes quiet. Now shake your hands vigorously, until you can feel your fingers tingle. Place your fingertips gently on your solar plexus and breathe in slowly and deeply. As you do so, imagine that you are breathing in a stream of pure white light through your nostrils, down into your solar plexus, and out into your fingertips.

When you have taken a complete breath, hold it, and slowly move your fingertips to your forehead. Gently touching the area between your eyebrows slowly expel your breath, imagining that you are breathing the pure white light out through your fingertips, filling your head completely with it. When your breath has been fully expelled, hold it, and return your fingertips to your solar plexus. Breathe the white light into your fingertips once again.

Repeat the process, but this time move your fingertips slowly to the throat area. Expel all your breath, watching the white light streaming through your fingertips and filling your throat with vitality and energy. When your breath has been fully expelled, return your fingertips to the solar plexus.

Repeat the process. This time move your fingertips slowly to the heart area, flooding the heart centre completely with white light. When your breath and the white light have been fully expelled, return your fingertips slowly to the solar plexus.

Repeat the whole process. This time carry the white light to the genital area, flooding it completely with energy and vitality. When your breath and the white light have been fully expelled, breathe in and out quickly, ballooning your cheeks, and blowing through your lips with each exhalation. At the same time sweep your open hands up and down the front of your face, chest and stomach areas. Do this four or five times, then sit quietly for five minutes, imbibing the moving energy which will appear to be vibrating through you.

This is an extremely invigorating exercise, and one which you will find beneficial in activating the main chakras. To gain the most benefit from it however, the exercise should be practised morning and evening.

In theory, the movements of the chakras should alternate from clockwise to anti-clockwise down the body, beginning with the brow centre, which itself should move with a clockwise motion. The base chakra should show an anti-clockwise movement. Incidentally, the chakra system of the female is usually the opposite way around, starting with an anti-clockwise movement at the brow centre, and concluding with a clockwise motion in the base centre.

Although it is believed that a healthy, well-balanced person should have a correctly vibratory aligned chakra system with alternated movements, this may not always be the case, because the chakras do change polarity throughout the day. This change may occur as a result of fatigue, stress, concentration, diet, etc. None the less, there is no reason why the chakras cannot be stimulated into activity and controlled by using the methods given here.

Incidentally, there is little use in dowsing (i.e. using a pendulum or dowsing rods to locate an energy source) the crown centre, as I have always found this to be unaffected by such treatments. In any case, the chakras with which we should be mostly concerned are, in fact, those which are associated directly with one's psychic abilities. Although the crown centre is an extremely important chakra, especially where man's spiritual evolution is concerned, it is my belief that it should not be included when considering, or carrying out, activation of the chakras, due to its sensitive and vulnerable nature.

 ## Exercise 8

For this experiment you will need to work with a partner. You will also need five small pieces of clear quartz crystal and a pendulum – preferably a crystal one, as these are more effective where chakra work is concerned.

First, lie flat on the floor, using a cushion to support your head. Your partner should place one quartz crystal beside each of your heels, one next to each shoulder, and one as close to the crown of the head as possible. Your partner will now dowse your chakras, using the pendulum, beginning with the brow centre.

The pendulum should be held as steadily as possible over the centre (chakra) at a distance of approximately 2in. (5cm.), until some movement has been effected in it. The amount of movement in the pendulum, which will swing either clockwise or anti-clockwise, will in fact signify how much activity is present in the chakra. Dowse all the chakras. Make a note of their condition so that you can chart any improvement.

At the conclusion of the exercise, continue to lie in the same position, with your hands resting lightly over the solar plexus, for at least 20 minutes. Breathe in a slow and rhythmical manner. Imagine powerful white energy swirling around you, passing through your body, from one crystal to the other. Visualize this energy moving through each of your chakras. Spend a few minutes on each chakra. See them vivified and coruscating with vibrant colours.

It is not enough to merely imagine the chakras coming alive with colour and energy, for these surges of energy must also be 'felt' and 'experienced' through your imagination. Remember: you are dealing with subtle energy forces, over which the mind has a greater influence than does the physical body. This energy needs to be visualized, focused on and mentally controlled in order to achieve the most effective and positive results.

It is quite usual to feel extremely tired when the exercise is over. It is important that a period of rest be taken now to enable positive results to be achieved.

There would be little use in dowsing the chakras again immediately after the exercise, because time is needed for the energy to circulate through the system, and for the results to be seen. When you feel fully refreshed your partner will dowse the chakras once more, repeating the exercise and recording any changes in activity in the chakras.

The mouth can often feel quite parched as a result of this exercise, so drink a glass of fresh, clear water when the whole treatment has been completed. Before consuming the water, pour it from one vessel to another, backwards and forwards through the air, in order to revitalize it with the force known as *Prana*. I will discuss this energy in the next chapter.

chapter 3

PSYCHIC ENERGY AND THOUGHT POWER

OST PEOPLE HAVE only a superficial contact and relationship with the world in which they live, and are largely oblivious to the life that surrounds them. Developing one's psychic powers allows one to gain access to a whole new and beautiful dimension of the universe, thus making each and every experience seem like an exciting and mysterious adventure.

We are influenced in more ways than one by the world which surrounds us, and we become what and who we are as a result of the knowledge we acquire of it. We experience this world through our five senses; should any of these senses be impaired in any way, the knowledge and experience we have of this world would also be impaired and lessened as a consequence.

Our five senses are being used each moment of every day, enabling us to see, hear, touch, taste and smell the things of the world in which we live. But we really only know a minute part, in comparison with what exactly there is to be known of this world. Few people are truly aware of what complexities of consciousness are actually involved in one's encounters with the world that surrounds us. Once the psychic faculties have been activated, access is gained, often unwittingly, to an abundance of information of the world surrounding you – both objects and people.

Personally, I do not subscribe to the old saying "A little knowledge is a dangerous thing". On the contrary, it is, I believe, your obligation to search and obtain what knowledge you can. I would say that a little knowledge is certainly far better than none, that is, as long as it is correct, and it works for you.

Whatever your reason for wanting to develop psychic powers, the responsibility for such a profound transformation ultimately lies with you. You must therefore fully understand its implications and possibilities. Once development begins to take place nothing in your life will ever be quite the same again. The whole concept of your life will change quite dramatically, and the emotional highs and lows that you experienced in the past, will be a mere shadow of the highs and lows that you will experience in the present and the future. It is a fallacy to believe that psychic powers will exempt you from pain and suffering simply because you are privy to knowledge which is denied to others.

I am often reminded of the wise words of mystic and dramatist Maurice Maeterlinck:

> *The wise man too must suffer, and suffering forms a constituent part of his wisdom. He shall suffer in the flesh, in the heart, and in the soul. And being near to mankind – no, being nearer to God as ever the wise man must be, the sufferings of others are his, in that his nature is far more complete than his brothers.*

Let us now consider 'thought power' and the concept of *psychic energy*. Psychic powers are all concerned with learning to control and direct such energy.

The word 'Prana' is used in Eastern philosophy to designate all energy in the universe. *Prana* is in fact the principle responsible for the maintenance of life in the physical body. It is the subtle agent which integrates the cells into a whole. *Prana* is all-pervading, and is to be found in everything having life, and of course everything possesses life to a greater or lesser degree. It is in the air that we breathe, it is in the water that we drink. It can be found working through all forms and degrees of matter, and yet, although *Prana* exists in all these things, it is, in fact, completely independent of them.

When the physical body is depleted in *Prana*, illness or disease results. Should *Prana* cease to be present in the physical body, death would immediately occur. It must, therefore, be understood that *Prana* has a specific part to play in the manifestation of life, and is, in more ways that one, responsible for it.

Prana is such a dynamic force that to be aware of its very existence is to be more than half-way to gaining access to its powerful universal reservoir. It sustains and perpetuates the very life in everything, and gives force and power to our thoughts and the way in which we think. It can infuse life into our thoughts, and enables us to propel them in any direction we choose, distance no object, for of course *thoughts are living things*. The stronger the thought, the more energy with which one charges that thought. The more energy present with each thought, the longer that thought will persist in the psychic space.

This concept was known to the ancient Egyptians, who utilized this powerful force to create centres of energy to protect the tombs of their great kings. These forces are probably still in existence today, silently protecting those tombs still as yet undiscovered.

Working on the premise that 'thoughts are living things', the thoughts which we create with a specific mission in mind are automatically infused with *Prana*, which propels them to do our bidding.

Most of the thoughts that are discharged during the course of the day however, such as 'What shall I cook for dinner?' 'It looks like rain', 'I'll have to pick the children up from school', have little or no force behind them. They dissolve and are quickly absorbed by the psychic space, to be resolved back into the ether. But those strong emotions which exploit and control our thoughts and mental energies, whether with fear or joy, happiness or sadness, love or hate, are immediately enveloped and infused with streams of *Prana*, propelling our thoughts and lending them wings.

In fact, we are continually peopling our own private portion of space by the way in which we think, and we are constantly being pulled along by those thought forces which we have created previously. As a direct consequence, nature always works towards the gratification of our most secret desires. You only have to look at how difficult it is to pull yourself out of depression, and to be more positive when problems have crowded in upon you. when things go wrong in your life it is very difficult, if not impossible, to fight back against circumstances. However, before one's circumstances can change, one must transform the way in which one thinks.

This concept applies not only to the spiritual life, but also to the mental, moral and physical lives. Once you are able to comprehend the fundamental principles underlying the concept of psychic energy and thought power, it is easy to see exactly what powers lie within you.

During the course of a normal day you probably touch thousands of objects without being aware of it. Things around the home and in the workplace which are handled and touched by you therefore possess tiny particles of your personal energies – minute particles of you.

Although the many things which you touch during the day are superficially encountered, and are probably therefore 'over-printed' with the vibrations of many other people, personal items such as jewellery, clothing, even domestic objects, may be strongly impregnated with your own energies.

By simply holding a personal item belonging either to someone living, or perhaps to someone who has long since died, it is possible to psychically 'read' its vibratory history, rather like flicking through the pages of a book. Although it takes time to perfect such an ability, I know of no more effective method of cultivating the psychic ability of clairvoyance. This method of 'reading' articles is called 'psychometry'. Although, strictly speaking, psychometry can only be used to glean information pertaining to the past and the present of those to whom the articles belong, or have belonged, I have known the information thus obtained to be extremely accurate.

On occasion psychometry can be used as a 'bridge', to enable the 'reader' to make contact with someone in the spirit world and to give concrete evidence of that person's continued existence.

A psychic will often ask a 'sitter' to hand them an item of personal jewellery to use as a sort of focal point, to help them make a 'connection' with that person. Quite often the information given by the psychic does not come from the item of jewellery, and may, in fact, have nothing whatsoever to do with it. But there are others who rely solely upon their ability to 'psychometrize', and without this skill they may find that they can do nothing. This, however, is down to training rather than to their lack of ability.

Psychometry not only helps to heighten one's sensitivity to the vibratory atmosphere of objects and people; it is also extremely effective in the development and cultivation of concentration, and this is of great importance where psychic work is concerned.

Psychometry is an ideal tool, and a useful and very effective means of improving one's psychic ability. However, one should not come to depend upon it totally. Use it, by all means, but use it along with other methods and as an integral part of your daily training programme.

 ## Exercise 9

Ask your friends to bring along items of jewellery belonging to people you have not known. Before you begin, sit quietly for a few minutes, until the mind is calm and you feel relaxed.

Ask someone to hand you an article. Hold the article gently with your fingertips. At first, do not try to achieve anything other than allowing your mind to blend with the article in your hand. Use both hands, and as many of your fingers as possible in the exercise.

When you feel calm, and your mind is quiet, try to feel that you have almost become the article, so completely have you blended with it. Examine all its qualities – its weight, texture, shape, even its temperature. You may not have any control over the psychic impressions which will pass spontaneously through your mind. Should this be the case, read them as they come, speaking them aloud, allowing your friend to record exactly what you say.

It is extremely important not to question or analyse anything that comes to you. The impressions may be fleeting and may be vague images, feelings or impressions. You may even sense a fragrance wafting over you, or feel a sequence of symbols passing through your mind. Psychometry can produce anything and everything.

Should the flow of impressions cease, mentally ask the article questions, for example, 'To whom did the ring or watch belong?' 'Where and when was it bought?', 'Are they dead?' 'How did they die?' Ask for names, dates and descriptions. Try to be adventurous with your questions. After all, you have nothing to lose and everything to gain.

Do not make this experiment laborious. Trying to force it merely defeats the object. If nothing at all comes to you it may well be that you need to try a different article. Experiment with as many objects as possible. Some people condition themselves into believing that they can only psychometrize certain objects. This is a fallacy: once the ability has been developed anything at all can be psychometrized.

Remember: psychometry is merely a useful tool. Although it can certainly produce very accurate information, once you have mastered the ability you will realize that you are most certainly capable of achieving much more.

Should you achieve positive results from psychometry and, therefore, feel comfortable enough to include it in your training programme, I believe it would be a good idea to also include a 'scrying' technique – which will encourage your psychic visual response mechanism to develop.

Although often treated with cynicism and disdain, I strongly recommend that you obtain a good quality crystal ball to aid you in your training programme. It is true to say that crystal balls usually conjure up ideas of a mysterious Gypsy Rose Lee-type figure sitting in a booth in a seaside resort, but I would ask you not to discount it as a possibility. The crystal ball has been an effective method of divination, used by seers for thousands of years. If it worked for them it can certainly work for you.

 ## Exercise 10

Having placed your crystal ball comfortably upon its pedestal, stand it on a table over which you have placed a covering of black velvet. This helps to reduce any light reflection, making it easier to concentrate. The lighting in your room must be subdued. Try to make the atmosphere as pleasant as possible. I would suggest burning some incense, and perhaps playing some soft background music.

Having set the scene, sit as comfortably as possible, with the crystal ball as close to eye level as is necessary. Simply gaze at it, ignoring any particles of light that may have found their way into the crystal. At first it is important not to blink, or to move your gaze away from the crystal. Try not to be distracted as your eyes inevitably begin to move out of focus. When you feel that you can no longer stare at the crystal ball without clearing your eyes, very slowly close them. Sit for a few moments, allowing the after image of the crystal to come into your mind's eye. Continuing to sit quietly, attune your mind to the crystal. Send thoughts to it: 'allow me to see', 'allow me to see'.

Once your mind has become completely relaxed and attuned to the vibrations of the crystal ball, open your eyes and return your gaze to it. As with the previous exercises, do not make this a labour, or you will merely defeat the object, which is, of course, to 'see' astral pictures. Continue to gaze at the crystal ball, blinking to clear your eyes when necessary. Try not to think of any one particular thing, or allow your thoughts to wander from the crystal.

At this point, *beware*. It is the time when most people become a little impatient, thinking that nothing is going to happen. But with crystal gazing, more than any other form of divination, a patient, determined attitude is definitely needed, and your patience will most certainly be rewarded with some interesting results.

Eventually, the interior of the crystal ball will appear to sparkle with a sort of green effervescence, full of movement. This will gradually subside, giving way to a slowly descending dark shadow which, as it falls, will cover the crystal ball completely. Your patience will be tested at this point, as the shadow may remain there, over the ball, for quite some time.

However, if you restrain your impatience and simply continue to 'watch', the shadow, or 'dark veil' as it is often called, will eventually begin to rise, uncovering the crystal ball, leaving it bright and alive. At first you will see nothing, although there will appear to be a bright light shining from within the crystal.

Eventually, pictures will appear in the crystal ball – landscapes, faces, and often beautiful colours. These images will have no great significance at first, and will not be familiar to you. It will take some time for your astral vision to be developed, but in the meantime you must not allow yourself to become disheartened, and must continue to practice with the crystal ball as often as time will permit.

While gazing at the crystal ball it is quite common for the gazer to 'see' images and light forms in their peripheral field of vision. These forms may appear to dance about you, but as soon as you move your eyes from the crystal to look at them, they simply disappear.

 # Exercise 11

Once the art of scrying has been mastered, and you feel quite confident that it is working for you, you may like to try reading the crystal ball for someone else, preferably a friend.

Ask the person to hold the crystal ball gently in their hands for a few moments, moving it up to touch their forehead as they make a few wishes or silent requests. Take the ball from them and return it to its pedestal. With your hands still cupped around it, begin to gaze at the crystal as you did for yourself.

You may find that pictures appear almost immediately, without any effervescence or dark veil, or you may have to go through the whole procedure again. Whatever the case, once the art has been mastered, I guarantee that you will be pleased with the results.

Remember: the art of scrying can take some time to develop. You may be one of the lucky ones however, and be fortunate enough to obtain positive results almost immediately.

A sensitive person is certainly far more susceptible to the subtle impulses of a psychically charged atmosphere than a non-sensitive person. Such sensitive people may often find themselves being constantly, and unknowingly, invaded by invisible psychic forces. However, not all of those invisible forces are of a negative nature. On the contrary. The sensitive person is also open to the influencing powers of positive, loving vibrations, also created, like the negative forces, by minds past and present.

I have already explained that we are constantly peopling our own private portion of space by the way we think, and that we are continually being pulled along by the thoughts and desires we have previously set in motion. Furthermore, the thoughts and desires that we discharge during the course of our lifetime are in turn pulled towards the thoughts and desires set in motion by other people. Collectively they form 'thought strata' in the psychic atmosphere, and they influence the minds of all those with a similar vibration.

Districts, towns, cities, countries and even nations are permeated with the thoughts and desires of all those who live or have lived there. A nation struck by famine, drought, poverty or war is influenced by the vibratory thought forces which envelope it, rather like clouds hovering in the atmosphere, charging and perpetuating the anguish of those who live there, making it virtually impossible for them ever to be free from their never-ending plight. The same principles and laws which operate in the psychic lives of a nation struck by famine or war also operate in a nation blessed with peace, happiness and wealth.

On a much smaller scale, the thoughts and desires of people past and present determine the psychic atmosphere of a building. The thoughts of those who live, or have lived there, psychically impregnate the subtle structure of the house, in time creating a living atmospheric personality, which represents the minds of all those who have, and who still, reside within its walls. One often experiences this psychic atmosphere when entering an old building. You may be immediately overwhelmed either by its warmth and friendliness, or perhaps by its coldness and unhappiness.

Although most people have experienced this sort of phenomenon at some time, a psychic person is always open to it and can, on occasion, be deeply affected by it. A psychic can also be strongly affected by other people's feelings and attitudes towards them. The developing psychic must therefore take measures to safeguard themselves from 'psychic attack', as this can, if allowed to persist, lead to a deterioration in their health. A 'psychic attack' does not necessarily have to be intentional to have an effect upon the sensitive mind. Hate, jealousy or malice secretly directed towards the psychic can wash over his or her aura like waves of electricity, temporarily altering his or her magnetic vibratory energy field and, if strong enough, causing him or her to feel depressed, out of phase, and possibly completely disorientated.

The effects of such an attack are, however, largely transitory. Should there be no real, rational reason for it – i.e. the victim is innocent – it will eventually be redirected, to return to the sender with a force far greater than that with which it was first dispatched. We would do well to remember the ancient precept, 'Curses and blessings come home to roost'; that is, like will always attract like.

Psychic work can certainly lower one's general resistance, making one susceptible to all sorts of minor ailments. An undisciplined psychic may be prone to depression, and if of a nervous disposition to begin with they may eventually find themselves more so, if precautionary measures are not taken. A healthy, well-balanced diet should be included in your training programme, along with plenty of fresh air and exercise, and a period in the day for turning off completely and relaxing.

You must learn to respect your psychic abilities, and never abuse them. Do not be persuaded to use them as a party piece. Should you persist in abusing, or over-using your abilities, they will certainly cease to be as effective, and will cause you psychological distress at a later date.

Some of the most effective methods of preventing loss of vitality are also some of the most simple. Do not underestimate their effectiveness because of their simplicity.

When one is stressed or anxious, or perhaps recovering from a bout of flu some other debilitating illness, the breathing becomes shallow and quick and the heart beats fast, causing even more loss of vitality. By relaxing the body as completely as one can, and breathing in a specific rhythmical way, it is possible to restore the body's vitality, thereby aiding recovery.

 # Exercise 12

The effects of this exercise will prove beneficial, even for the person with no interest in psychic development, and will help to revitalize the brain in times of stress.

Sit comfortably by an open window, or better still (weather permitting), in the garden. First, ascertain your normal heartbeat by placing your fingers on your pulse. Sit quietly for a few moments, familiarizing yourself with your heart rhythm.

The vibratory rhythm of your body must correspond with the vibratory frequency of each heartbeat. Breathing with a specific rhythm controls the flow of energy (*Prana*) into the body, and prevents any unnecessary loss of that energy, which may often occur in the case of stress or illness. In this particular exercise we are working to a rhythm of 6/3. When you feel quite calm and comfortable, breathe in for the count of six heartbeats; hold it for the count of three; breathe out for the count of six; and count three between breaths. Repeat this process over about eight or ten minutes.

For the next part of the exercise clasp your hands in front of you, across your solar plexus. This 'seals the tap', and prevents loss of *Prana*. Still keeping your eyes closed, breathe in with the same slow and easy rhythm, visualizing streams of coral- or pink-coloured energy passing in through your nostrils, down through your lungs and into the solar plexus. Holding your breath for the count of three, allow the vibrant energy to circulate around the solar plexus in a clockwise motion. Then, infusing it with the negative colour grey, or even black, expel it to the count of six. Repeat the exercise until you feel revitilized. Then sit quietly, with the eyes closed, allowing the *Prana* to circulate.

It is quite usual to experience some tingling, either on the face and forehead, or in the hands and fingertips. This is one of the ways in which currents of Pranic energy manifest, and it confirms that the exercise has been done correctly.

Once you have familiarized yourself with your own bodily rhythm, it is not necessary to count the heartbeats with your breathing. You should eventually allow your mind to drift from both the counting and your breathing until you become completely unconscious of both.

This exercise is ideal for 'recharging the batteries' after a tiring day at work, or when you are preparing for a job interview, or going into some other stressful situation. It has the effect of sweeping the aura with *Prana* and infusing the chakra system with vitality, thereby boosting your reserves of psychic energy.

chapter 4

LOOKING FORWARD THROUGH TIME

*I*T IS PERHAPS only over the last fifteen years or so that science has made any real effort to comprehend the concept of time, to the extent that one notable scientist has had to rethink his theories about time and the possibility of travelling through it.

Time is one of those great mysteries that man has always found difficult to comprehend, although it has always held a great fascination for the writers of science fiction who have exploited the subject to the full, exciting and catching the imagination of millions of readers with stories of time travel and time exploration.

In fact, to enable man to live with time, he has arbitrarily divided it into a past, a present and a future. He restricts himself to within the confines of the past and the present, thinking the future to be beyond the range of his vision. He compartmentalizes the events that he has already experienced into the section of his memory labelled 'the past', and at times he apparently has great difficulty in dealing with the present, until that, too, is ready to be placed in the section labelled the past.

Man has little difficulty in recalling the past to the present, but he tends to perceive the future rather like a blind man wandering alone in some strange, mysterious land, almost as though he has an inherent dread of it.

Space, however, appears to present a far smaller problem to man. This, at least, seems to be more obvious to him, inasmuch as he is able to move more freely in space than he can in time. He can move forwards, backwards and sidewards in space, and now he has learned to move outwards and upwards, thus conquering the limitations imposed upon his predecessors, by designing and building flying machines and spacecrafts.

It would thus appear that science is now only just beginning to bring into reality the images, impressions and dreams of the science fiction writers of the last sixty years or more. Could it therefore be that the mind is truly the common denominator? Could each one of us be linked to the other, and could all in some way be connected to a universal reservoir, in which the past, the present and the future are experienced as one? Is it not a fact that the astronaut makes a mockery of time when he perceives the earth from a great height, with the nights, days and time differences of all the countries in the world visibly manifesting together, all at the same time?

We are most certainly limited, in more ways than one, by our brains and the way in which they have evolved. The rearrangement of a cerebral lobe, and the addition of a fine network of nerves to those which form our consciousness, would no doubt be all that is needed to make the future unfold itself before us, with the selfsame clarity and majestic amplitude as that with which the past is displayed upon the horizon of our memories.

Perhaps in the future man will have mastered the art of manipulating time, and travelling through it. If this is true, and the future has already happened, why has no one travelled back to inform us of what they know? Perhaps they have, and perhaps the past to which future man has travelled is not the present that we know and are experiencing at this moment in our time.

Perhaps the universe itself is not what it appears to our ephemeral minds. It is certainly multiplistic by its very nature, with worlds existing within worlds, each rising in a gradually ascending vibratory scale, from the lowest aspects of the physical world to the very highest of the spiritual realms.

Man, it would appear, is used to mentally looking in one direction, and that is to the past. He regards the future as being out of bounds, and is probably afraid of what he might see.

The future has always held a great fascination for man – a curious, and at times naive fascination, that was often exploited by the ancient seers and visionaries whom he would consult for information about his future. Needless to say, not all seers in ancient times were genuine. However, those who were had long since discovered a way of gaining access into that mysterious land of the future, even though some of the strange and weird methods of divination used by them in doing so would no doubt be ridiculed or frowned upon today.

However, some seers needed nothing at all to help them to see into the future, and would often appear to stare vacantly into space in order to glean the information they required.

Once your psychic ability has shown signs of manifesting, the art of 'staring' can be perfected with practice, and the ability to perceive the future developed in time.

It is possible that your psychic ability presently manifests as no more than strong intuitive feelings, and that you neither see nor hear anything which could be regarded as a psychic experience. You may also still have a lot of self-doubt regarding the possibility of your being psychic, and you may still discount any strong, extraordinary feelings which you experience, putting them down to intuition. However, you must understand that intuitive abilities manifest through the same faculties as do psychic abilities, and they are often all that remains in most people of the primitive mechanism of the survival faculty.

The devout sceptic denies the existence of psychic abilities, but will readily accept the existence of intuition, simply because it is traditionally accepted by society, while psychic abilities are not.

It would be extremely difficult to describe the taste of sugar to someone who has never tasted it, or to describe colour to a person who has been visually handicapped from birth. It is equally difficult to describe exactly what a psychic vision is like to a person who has never experienced one.

We have all experienced the natural phenomenon of day-dreaming – staring blankly into space as nebulous pictures pass, sometimes nostalgically, across our consciousness. But, while day-dreaming, how many times have pictures or images that you did not recognize floated across your mind? You therefore discounted them, putting them down to pure imagination.

The faculty responsible for the psychic ability of 'clairvoyance' manifests in various unexpected ways. The images produced through the process of day-dreaming also manifest from that same faculty, and can be developed and cultivated with the use of the same techniques. But what use would there be in developing the ability to day-dream, merely to recall pictures of one's past?

DEVELOP YOUR ABILITY TO DAY-DREAM INTO THE FUTURE

I have used the term 'day-dream' as an example, in order to help you understand exactly how most clairvoyant impressions appear. They can often be quite nebulous, even when the ability has been developed into a fine art. Even when one has undergone extensive training, and possesses an extremely accurate psychic ability, demonstrations of such powers must always be looked upon as purely experimental, because the results of such demonstrations are rarely consistent. However, practice does make it as perfect as it can be.

 Exercise 13

Take a piece of matt black cardboard, measuring approximately 2ft. (60cm.) square, and paint a white dot in the very centre. Then take a piece of white cardboard of the same size, in the centre of which you should paint a black dot. Prop up both cards in front of you, facing you and as near to eye level as possible. They should be at a distance of approximately 3ft. (90cm.) from you.

Spend a few moments relaxing, eyes closed, making the mind quiet. Breathe slowly and deeply, still with your eyes closed, allowing your stomach to rise as you breathe in, and to fall as you breathe out. Continue this for a few minutes.

Once you are perfectly relaxed, open your eyes and slowly move your gaze to the white dot in the centre of the black card. Focus your gaze on this dot, resisting the temptation to blink or to move your eyes away even for a moment, as this will defeat the object of the exercise. Should you find it impossible to gaze without blinking, then blink, but do not move your eyes away from the centre dot, even for a split second. When you can gaze no longer, close your eyes and place your hands over them. Wait for the after image to appear slowly in your mind's eye.

Watch the image float around your consciousness for a few moments, breathing in and out slowly and deeply, willing the image to become brighter and more clearly defined every time you breathe in. Retain this image in your mind's eye for a few moments, then turn your attention to the white card.

Open your eyes and allow your gaze to focus on the black dot in the centre of the white card. Repeat the staring process. As you gaze at the black dot, notice how the previous after image of the black card appears to be superimposed over the white card. Continue to gaze at the black dot, resisting any distraction you may feel from the previous after image. When you can no longer hold your gaze, slowly close your eyes and watch the new after image being introduced into your consciousness.

Continue this exercise for a maximum of 15 to 20 minutes, alternating cards as you repeat the process.

Practise this exercise at least three times a week, more if possible. This particular technique has the effect of stimulating the creative visual response mechanism, and eventually precipitating the clairvoyant ability.

The person who has no great difficulty in visualizing images and who can create pictures in the mind's eye with ease has a far greater chance of developing the ability of clairvoyance than does someone who cannot visualize. The process of clairvoyance involves creative energies and impulses from the imagery faculty. Artists, or anyone who works in a creative field, quite often possess potential psychic abilities, and they probably experience these in their work from time to time without even realizing it.

Exercise 14

This exercise should be practised with a partner in order to obtain the best positive results.

Use only the black card (see Exercise 13). Sit in front of the propped up black card and ask your partner to sit behind it. Place a cassette recorder beside you to record the whole experiment. Tell your partner to project a picture through the back of the black card to you, while you focus your gaze on the white dot. The projected picture can be anything at all, from a simple landscape to a complex geometric shape.

While gazing at the white dot you should allow your mind to remain passively empty, making no attempt to receive the picture your partner is sending. When you can no longer gaze at the dot, close your eyes and place the palms of your hands over them, watching the after image appear very slowly in your mind's eye. It is at approximately this point that your partner's mental impression should gradually become visible to you.

At first nothing may happen, but if you persevere with the experiment you will begin to receive vague impressions of a fragmented picture. Of course, you may not see anything very clearly, and may just be overwhelmed with vague sensations. Whatever you experience, you must voice it immediately. This often makes any impressions received grow stronger and much clearer.

If at first you are not successful, ask your partner to transmit another picture. In my experience the composition of the picture is not important. It can be anything from a simple image to an extremely complex pattern – it does not matter which. If the exercise is going to work, it will work just as well with an intricate design as with a single, solitary line.

Once you have mastered the technique, and developed a rapport with your partner, a telepathic relationship will become apparent in the results that you obtain.

By practising this sort of exercise, you will eventually discover your own technique and way of achieving the desired results.

Most people who show even the smallest interest in psychic matters often do so because of an experience which they themselves have had at some time or another, which has left them with the feeling that there is more to be developed. When cornered, even the most ardent cynic will admit that they have had an unusual psychic experience at some time.

The most common experience, and one which most people say they have had, is that of knowing of someone's death long before the news arrives. Or knowing the phone is going to ring before it does, and perhaps even knowing who the caller will be. These kinds of experience (precognitive experience) transcend the bounds of coincidence, particularly when they usually happen more than once.

I have often heard it said of psychics that they possess over-active imaginations, or that they are too sensitive. These accusations are correct on both counts. A strong, active imagination appears to be a prerequisite for the development of psychic abilities, and the stronger the abilities the more sensitive the psychic. I would hope that with the help of the exercises in this book you will be able to control your sensitivity, and learn to channel it in a positive way.

Furthermore, in order to develop your psychic abilities further, you must allow your imagination to work for you. To suppress it in any way will merely inhibit any latent psychic tendencies. You must, therefore, give your imagination its freedom, and allow your creative faculties to be active. The following exercise is an example of an experiment in which your imagination can be used. It may prove to you that there is an extremely fine line between what we know as the psychic faculty, and what we call imagination.

 ## Exercise 15

For this experiment you will need to work with a partner.

Find an empty box with a lid.

Close your eyes and sit quietly.

Ask your partner to place a small object of their choice inside the box and close the lid. (Obviously, you must not know what object your partner has chosen.)

Visualize the box surrounded by a very bright white light. Imagine yourself breathing the bright white light deep into your lungs and into your solar plexus. Continue to focus all your attention on the image of the box in your mind. Look upon the box as a conscious entity, full of life, to whom you can speak. If it helps you, make it into a sort of cartoon character with features, such as eyes, a mouth and legs etc. Animate the box in your mind, and let it be willing to both listen and talk to you. Ask it to reveal its contents to you. Wait for the answer. No matter how ridiculous the answer seems, repeat it to your partner, who should tell you immediately whether or not you are correct.

Limit yourself to six attempts at discovering the box's contents. Should you not be successful by then, ask your friend to exchange the article for another.

If you have difficulty in picturing the box as an animated cartoon figure, focus all your attention on the image of the box in your mind. Slowly rotate it in your mind, and look at it from all angles – from each side, from the top, from the back, even from the bottom. Imagine yourself picking up the box to gauge its weight. While holding it in your hands see yourself lifting the lid and peering inside. You should tell your partner the first thing you see inside the box. Should you be correct, repeat the experiment with another article straight away.

It is important that you do not question how you obtained successful results in this exercise. Do not add doubt by saying it was achieved by guess work. How you do it is not important. If you achieve a success rate of six or more out of ten, apparently by guessing, then that is the way it will work for you. Accurate information is often obtained by psychics who appear to guess. Once a psychic ability develops, the way in which it works for you should not be questioned, as long as it is a reliable method which produces positive results.

Precognitive abilities – glimpses of the future – which I touched on above, are more common than one might imagine. They often display themselves as overwhelming feelings of apprehension –

perhaps a strong, intuitive feeling regarding a stranger, or an approaching situation. Sometimes we are 'impressed' to act on impulse, or we perhaps feel pleasurable anticipation about an approaching opportunity, or about a situation that, to everyone else, appears quite depressing.

These strong feelings may only occasionally be experienced, and they often come without any preliminary warning. None the less, they are very real to the person who experiences them, and should therefore be accepted as one of probably many psychic abilities which they possess.

LOOKING FORWARD

Even though you may now possess a fairly strong and reliable psychic ability, you may still not yet have developed, or mastered, the art of looking into the future. You may have imposed limitations upon yourself by only experimenting with those methods whose results can be immediately confirmed.

Before attempting to develop the ability to look into the future, you must try and understand that by controlling the mind, instead of allowing the mind to control you, you can influence the dynamic forces of the future. You can control circumstances and events before they actually happen, and watch them unfold across your consciousness, as though viewing a television programme which nobody else can see.

This is rather different from precognition, although I do not doubt that the faculty through which precognition manifests is also responsible for the gift of prophesying the future.

In theory, precognition and prophetic vision are the same, but with one small difference. Precognition is mostly involuntary, and the gift of prophecy, although it *can* happen spontaneously, can be controlled.

Before any attempt is made to develop the ability to prophesy the future, you should first have some understanding of the principles underlying the mechanics of awareness. Human awareness manifests at four different levels, and one's consciousness has an experience at all of these levels at some time or another, often without your even realizing it.

For instance, you may be driving home from work through rush-hour traffic. Mentally you are going over the day's stressful events, or perhaps you are preoccupied with the arrangements for the coming evening's dinner party. You suddenly become aware that you have parked your car in front of your house, and you have done so with no recollection of the journey you have just made.

It would almost seem as though, within us all, there is an 'automatic pilot' which takes over when we are out of control. The same can be said for when we are faced with an arduous task for the first time, one which demands a great deal of concentration. While our attention is focused entirely upon the job at hand we are oblivious to all else around us, and completely unaware of any sound or distraction. However, once the task has been mastered it can be brought under the control of our 'automatic pilot', and, if necessary, be carried out with little or no concentration.

The first and lowest level of human awareness is one which we all experience, all the time. Through this level we gain our knowledge of the world in which we live. The second level of awareness is also shared by everyone, but usually only in times of stress, anxiety, or activation of the survival reflex – that is, when we are under threat of danger.

However, the examples I have given above are in the extreme. In actuality, this second level of awareness is also the aspect of consciousness in which we are capable of achieving extraordinary things. It is subdivided into two aspects: the first takes control of our anxieties and the need to survive, and the second appears to elevate our consciousness into and through the third level of awareness, so bringing about a greater realization of the impulses received from the fourth level of awareness, which is that of spirit.

We are limited by terminology in our definitions of these levels of awareness, so I will refer to them as *physical awareness, instinctive awareness, intellectual awareness*, and *spiritual awareness*.

Intellectual awareness represents the thinker in man. It is the level at which he enquires and analyses. It represents the 'I' consciousness, through which man seeks knowledge and expression. Depending on the degree of consciousness he has of the fourth level (that of spiritual awareness), the intellectual level of awareness can be extremely cold, arrogant, self-opinionated and cynical. At its more positive, the intellectual level of awareness brings man ideas and makes him an innovator. Through this level the higher spiritual, or real self, can express its feelings, bringing into the man's consciousness spiritual revelations, light and inspiration.

Through the fourth level, spiritual awareness, man experiences divine inspiration and that closeness to God in that place of light. Having experienced a level of spiritual awareness, man realizes that words alone will not in any way represent what he has discovered. His tongue appears ineffectual, almost as though some secret command has been given, willing him to silence.

The spiritual level of awareness does not in any way overpower the third level of intellectual awareness; it simply transcends it, passing down to it the experiences encountered in its own levels. These are yet again explored at the level of intellectual awareness, whereupon man analyses and reasons about them.

Before attempting to use your psychic powers to prophesy the future, you need first of all to experience the various levels of awareness at which they are acquired, to enable the route of entry to be reliably accessible. In this way results can be successfully achieved each time.

 # Exercise 16

This exercise has been designed to enable you to experience varying degrees of emotional, mental and spiritual awareness. It is often productive of suppressed emotions, by making you aware of old and deeply buried fears, anxieties and sorrows. It is more an exercise in self-awareness than of meditation, and often promotes a greater realization of the soul and its independence of the body.

To achieve the desired results, the exercise must be practised with total dedication. Allow it to create for you a sanctuary, or inner sanctum, into which you can retreat when seeking peace and serenity.

Find a comfortable chair and relax for a few moments with your eyes closed. Make your mind as quiet as you possibly can.

Breathe slowly and deeply for a few moments, relaxing as you do, and focusing your thoughts totally upon yourself. Silently, say to yourself, 'My body is not me. I merely reside in it. I may leave it at any time I wish, but I must return to it when the exercise is concluded.'

Repeat this three or four times, fixing it firmly in your mind. Then begin.

Imagine yourself standing on the worn stone steps of a beautiful old monastery. Look down at the steps and notice the texture and colour of the stone, and the uneven cracks running through them. The ornately carved oak doors of the monastery slowly open, and as you look up you see the aged, frail figure of a monk standing on the threshold. Your eyes take in the heavy brown cloth of his habit, and the pale skin of his elderly, wrinkled face. He smiles at you and raises a hand in a welcoming gesture.

Follow the monk as he turns and walks through the doorway into the monastery. As the doors slowly close behind you they bring a veil of stillness down around you, and you become aware of the quiet, calm atmosphere of the monastery. Follow the old man as he makes his way slowly down a shadowy passageway, lit only by flickering lamps strategically placed on the stone walls either side of you. Dark shadows reach across the floor in front of you. Your heart quickens in anticipation as you hasten to keep up with the old monk, whose shuffling footsteps echo off the walls. You emerge into a huge, round, brightly lit hall. The high, domed, stained glass ceiling allows a cascade of colour to pool down upon the marble, mosaic floor, which appears to glisten and sparkle as if it, too, is made of glass. As you look around you notice that the walls of the hall appear translucent. They shimmer like mother-of-pearl. You notice several monks moving contemplatively around you, chanting to an accompaniment of chimes. For a moment you remain still, listening to the chanting.

Smiling, your elderly guide gestures towards a doorway on the other side of the hall. You obediently walk across the cool marble floor towards it. By the time you reach the door it is already open. Through the doorway you can see a narrow wooden staircase leading upwards. Move towards it, and stand for a moment at the foot of the stairs. Watch the sunlight stream in through a high window on the landing above you, throwing shards of bright light across the floor and walls. In the distance you can still hear the rhythmic chanting of the monks.

Begin to ascend the stairs, one step at a time, feeling a rush of excitement as you climb higher and higher. Follow the staircase as it turns to the left. A few more steps and you find yourself standing alone on the first landing, gazing curiously down the long narrow passageway in front of you. There is a sweet fragrance in the air, and a sense of peace and well-being overwhelms you. You become aware of an extremely strong, familiar feeling of having been here before.

As you look along the passageway you notice three doors on the left side and two doors on the right. At the very end of the passage, facing you, there is one door. Pause for a few moments before moving to the door of your choice.

Before choosing a door it is important to realize that at this level you are given the opportunity to deal with all those negative, self-destructive thoughts and emotions. You are now at the second level, or what I have called 'instinctive awareness', and it is important that, upon entering the room of your choice, you either immediately rearrange it to your liking, or simply remove an item of furniture, or anything else you find unpleasant, from the room. Before you leave the room you *must* feel comfortable with it.

Now, enter the room of your choice, and close the door gently behind you. Have a good look around. Observe the walls, the windows, the furniture, the rugs on the floor. Sit down on a chair for a few moments, imbibing the atmosphere. Then change anything you do not feel comfortable with.

Now you must leave. Move towards the door. Pause for a moment to have a last look around the room. Open the door and move into the corridor, closing the door behind you as you leave. Before moving away from the room, mentally prepare yourself for the next level – that of 'intellectual awareness'. This is the level at which ideas will come to you. You will feel strongly inspired at that level, and may even decide that you do not wish to go any further. Should this be the case, do not in any way question the apprehension you feel; simply leave, and return to the ground floor, the first level.

Now continue along the corridor to the staircase at the end. Climb the stairs very slowly, allowing your hand to brush against the cool stone wall. It feels solid and secure beneath your fingers. Once again the feeling of anticipation rushes through you. Within moments you reach the next level.

At the top of the stairs you move directly into a small study. There are shelves and shelves of books around the walls, and a desk, upon which you notice a writing quill resting in an inkwell. There is a blank piece of parchment lying next to it. A fire is burning brightly in the fireplace, which is surrounded by a beautifully designed mantel. You can feel the heat from the fire. Sit in the armchair in front of it for a few moments, allowing the peace and serenity of the study to wash over you. At the same time reflect upon your visit to the monastery, and your reason for coming.

This level is often productive of symbols, ideas and overwhelming feelings. Make your mind completely open to them. Rise from the chair and move over to the desk. Take the quill firmly in your hand and scribble on the parchment the first word that comes to mind. Have a good look around the room. Feel contemplative, mentally alert, and completely open to the impulses from the next level – that of spiritual awareness. Make a mental note of what you have written on the parchment, and move away from the desk.

Leave the study and walk back towards the head of the staircase. Your eyes search for the way up to the next level (spiritual awareness). There do not appear to be any stairs up to the next level. Stand for a few moments contemplating the way forward.

You suddenly realize that the only access route to the fourth level is through your own imagination.

Imagine yourself standing and holding out your arms, while staring upwards. Imagine an intense white light above you, as if shining through the ceiling. Allow that bright light to slowly descend and envelop you. Feel the light all around you, inter-penetrating every cell of your body. You feel totally disorien-tated and lose all sense of your surroundings. Almost at once you feel the bright light gradually fading into nothingness, and you find yourself standing in a beautifully lit sanctuary, in the centre of which there is a comfortable armchair. Sit down in the chair and enjoy the peace, the quiet and the solitude. Feel totally at peace in that sanctuary, allowing your imagination to create whatever it wishes. Be aware of every aspect of your surroundings, and of the sweet fragrance wafting over you in the stillness. Remain there for as long as you wish. It may be that you will lose all sense of time, for time does not exist at the fourth level, where all the answers lie.

When you are ready to leave, simply allow the quiet sanc-tuary to slowly fade from your consciousness. Find yourself standing at the top of the stairs, on the third level.

Move slowly down the stairs, taking in your surroundings as you descend, eventually reaching the second level. Without pausing, continue to move down the stairs to the ground floor and the first level. Pass through the small door into the spacious round room with the domed ceiling and the mosaic floor. There you are greeted by the elderly monk. This time, pay particular attention to his aged, lined face. Notice his eyes, which are warm and friendly. Feel secure and safe with him, for next time you must greet him as an old friend.

Follow the old man across the mosaic floor, this time paying attention to the intricate detail in the design of the patterns on the floor. Follow him back along the shadowy passageway until you reach the monastery doors. Open them, and move outside into the cool, fresh breeze that gently touches your hair. Turn and bid your guide farewell. Mentally ask him if you may return. He nods his answer with a smile, and then closes the doors.

Breathe very slowly and deeply a few times, and dissolve the exercise from your mind. Relax for a few moments in your chair.

This has been an exercise in awareness, and it is one which must be used as often as possible in order to obtain the best results. You will find whatever you desire to know of the future at the fourth level. However, it will take time and patience before you achieve the desired results. Once the energies have been created in the exercise, your prophetic intuition will begin to produce glimpses of anything you wish to see.

Once you have developed an affinity with the exercise, and you have come to understand it fully, you can begin to explore its possibilities in a more confident way. Having confidence in the exercise, and allowing yourself to become totally involved with it, is of primary importance. However, the most difficult result to accept and to deal with can often be the sudden rush of feelings which eventually surface from the bottom of the pool of emotion. Although the exercise appears to be quite simple, do not underestimate its many benefits.

In the early days, when I used this exercise as an integral part of my training programme, I noticed that my dreams became more lucid, often producing meaningful prophetic symbols, which helped me immensely with my own life. This changed much later on, once I discovered a positive method of using my dreams as a means of answering the questions I asked of the future. It will all of course take time. But I am quite certain that successful results will be achieved once you have established a relationship with this exciting exercise in awareness.

chapter 5

GROUP AND SOLO WORK

S OME PEOPLE MAY feel that the support of a group around them can be of great benefit when endeavouring to develop their psychic abilities. The encouragement received from a group can be a great source of strength, as well as a confidence booster, particularly when the positive results you are seeking are not forthcoming.

The one thing that can cause some disappointment, however, when working in a group, is that every one of its members expects total dedication, support and encouragement from the rest of the group – something which is simply not possible.

The group must be in total agreement about helping the one whose psychic development is the most advanced, and who, therefore, needs the group's collective energies to be focused totally on them. The envy and jealousy to which this often gives rise can create an extremely destructive force, which will work against those with aspirations towards the development of psychic powers.

But, in saying this, group activity *can* work, and can produce some brilliant psychics, particularly when all the members of the group have an affinity with each other, and are therefore able to work together in total harmony.

Although working by yourself does have its advantages, and quite often its rewards, working in a group brings a much greater sense of freedom to your own developing powers, and the combined energies of the group can often bring about some startling results. Working through one's development within a group, as opposed to working alone, calls for a completely different approach, even though most of the methodology used to precipitate psychic abilities is the same.

Results often appear to manifest far sooner with a group approach to development. Perhaps the greatest danger here is that individually, each member may come to rely far too much on the collective energies of the group, and may, therefore, experience some difficulties when the time arrives for them to work alone. To prevent this from happening it is advisable for each member to be given a working programme, especially designed for them to use alone. This enables the developing psychic to be independent, self-sufficient, and able to rely upon their own energies.

I would suggest that each member works through their own programme, by themselves, the same number of times a week (or month) that the group meets. It is better, but by no means essential, to have an even number of members in your group and, if possible, an equal number of men and women, in order to create and maintain a well-balanced flow of energy. Psychic energy can be created very easily by a group who work well together. This energy can be used for specific reasons, such as healing, or for effecting telekinetic activity, i.e. causing objects to move without any physical contact with them. It can also be created by a group for the purpose of precipitating each individual's chakra system, or, by the use of a specific exercise, such energy can be created and then transferred from one person to the other, producing some extraordinary results.

 ## Exercise 17

Some years ago I designed this exercise for use in a group I was leading. I call the exercise 'The spiralling mantra', for reasons that will become apparent to you later on. It creates such power that everyone is affected, both those in the group and those who remain outside it. The spiralling mantra is very effective in the revitalization of the chakra system. It somehow energizes the collective aurae of the group, promoting alertness and sharpness of the senses.

Step One

Form a circle (using chairs) with, if possible, males and females seated alternately. Should equal numbers of males and females not be present, don't worry; just seat them as best you can.

Each person's left hand should be turned palm up, and their right hand palm down. Touch hands with the person next to you, until the complete circuit has been formed, all around the circle.

With eyes closed, the group should now spend five or ten minutes breathing slowly and deeply, keeping to a group rhythm. Begin to imagine a pulsating stream of pure white light passing around the circle, flowing from one person to the next, along the arms and through the hands.

By now you should already have noticed a difference in the room temperature. Group members may also begin to experience some tingling in their hands.

Step Two

The group should now begin to chant a specific mantra. Although most words with symbolic meaning will create energy when chanted rhythmically, the word to be used here is 'Ksham'. The 'K' is silent in the word 'Ksham' – it should, therefore, be chanted as 'Sham'. This is quite a powerful mantra and is used to create and release the inherent forces within 'Ajna', the brow centre. The group should not chant the mantra exactly in unison. It should be slightly staggered, leaving about one second between each person's intonation.

Group member one will begin the chant. Inhaling a deep breath he will chant the word Ksham on his exhalation, continuing the sound until all his breath has been fully expelled.

One second after group member one begins the chant, the group member on his left (group member two) will also begin, and will chant the mantra in the same way.

One second after group member two begins the chant, the group member on his left will also begin, and so on. In this way the chant will travel clockwise around the circle, each member chanting the mantra Ksham in turn.

Sound your voices as loudly as possible, and remember to keep your hands in the same position.

Each participant should continue the sound until all the breath has been fully expelled. They should then wait until the sound has completed the circuit and returned to them. Then, inhaling a deep breath, they should repeat the chant one second after the person on their right has begun it. Continue the chanting for ten minutes – more if possible – and then, on a given instruction, allow it to fade away.

When the group has fallen silent each person should remain still, in the same position, with their eyes closed, allowing the energy to circulate from one to the other, around the circle.

The effects of the spiralling mantra are quite spectacular. I have never known it not to be performed successfully. It creates an incredible amount of energy, from which everyone feels some benefit.

WHAT IS THE PURPOSE OF THE SPIRALLING MANTRA?

The main purpose of the spiralling mantra is to create energy within the group. Once created, however, the energy cannot be left. It must be discharged, preferably with a specific mission in mind.

It can be discharged for the purpose of cleansing the atmosphere in a building where there is a great deal of negative energy. This negative energy could perhaps manifest as some disturbing psychic activity, such as a poltergeist, or anything which disrupts the equilibrium of the atmosphere. The energy created by the spiralling mantra can be extremely effective in the process of restoring normality to a psychically disrupted home, or even the atmosphere pervading a village.

Once this powerful force has been created within the group it may be channelled into healing, either for a particular group of people, or, on a much wider scale, to a nation where there is strife, disease or even war. Discharged over a period of time, this energy can effect specific changes, restoring the general health and vigour of those at whom it is directed. The transformation is often very subtle, but it can be quite spontaneous, particularly when the process is repeated regularly.

On a much smaller scale, two or even three people who are in need of healing can be seated in the centre of the circle while the chanting is taking place. During the process of chanting it is important that those seated in the centre keep their eyes closed. They should not cross their legs, and their hands should remain clasped in their laps in front of them. Those who receive the healing force in this way nearly always describe it as like sitting inside a huge bell. It is a pleasant sensation which, as the chanting swirls around them, makes them lose all sense of weight, and produces a feeling of complete disorientation.

Once the chanting has ceased a feeling of total calm settles over them. If they had previously been experiencing any pain, it usually disappears immediately. The 'patient' is often left feeling quite emotional. At the conclusion of the chanting there should be a period of stillness and silence, allowing the group, and those in the centre of the circle, to imbibe the spiralling force.

The exercise should be concluded with a few deep inhalations and exhalations of breath. The hands may then be withdrawn, thereby breaking the circuit. The group should now raise their arms in the direction of the 'patients' in the centre of the circle. With a final exhalation of breath, the energy must be discharged into the patients, through the group's outstretched arms.

Of course, you may chose to experiment with the spiralling mantra to discover your own way of working with it. Should your group be a small one, you may find it necessary to modify the exercise in some way, and perhaps even use a different mantra. As long as the group is comfortable with the mantra, and it is one you are all familiar with, you will find it just as effective.

Remember, use the spiralling mantra with respect and look upon it as a spiritual exercise. Do not underestimate its effectiveness, for it is an extremely powerful exercise, which holds great appeal for those who prefer the more ritualistic approach to healing. The spiralling mantra can be used as an integral part of a healing programme. Although this book is not specifically concerned with healing, it is a good idea to discharge surplus energy through the channel of healing.

Being too focused upon the development of one's psychic powers can cause an unhealthy buildup of psychic energy in one's personal atmosphere. The spiralling mantra is an ideal way of clearing such energy in a positive way.

You may also like to experiment with the following method, which is usually called 'battery healing', because of the way in which the healing force is created.

 # Exercise 18

This method can be used with as few as four people to create the healing battery. All you need is the group, and one other person designated to receive the healing.

Seat the 'patient' comfortably, eyes closed, hands resting lightly in their lap. They should be as relaxed as possible – if necessary, talk them through relaxation. When the 'patient' is calm and relaxed, the rest of the group should move their chairs into a semicircle in front of them, close enough to hold hands with the 'patient' and with each other.

Using the same process as with the spiralling mantra (Exercise 17), the group member on the patient's right should place his or her left hand, palm down, in the patient's hand, and then place their right hand, palm up, in the hand of the person on their right. Continue in the same way around the semicircle, until the final person places his or her right hand, palm down, in the patient's left hand, thus making the 'battery' complete.

At the very moment the circuit is completed, there is such a surge of power through it that nothing, except participation in the actual experience of the exercise, will suffice to describe the feeling. The whole group should attune their thoughts to the patient, keeping their breathing in phase with each other, the inhalations and exhalations as nearly in unison as possible. This rhythmic breathing should continue for the entire duration of the healing process, and only be allowed to cease when all hands have been released and the circuit broken.

Incidentally, this method of healing should not be confused with what is termed 'spiritual healing'. The technique of 'battery healing' is of a purely psychic nature, and is produced as a result of the combined energies of the group being channelled into the patient.

This form of healing is extremely effective in the case of inflammatory diseases, where there is much pain, and also in the treatment of nervous disorders. It is not to be considered as a curative treatment, but used more to restore the body's vitality, enabling its self-healing process to be normalized.

Again, as with the spiralling mantra, you may like to experiment with this method, and perhaps use it in a different way. Although the number of people taking part is of little importance, in my experience the more people involved in forming the battery, the better and more powerful the results.

 Exercise 19

You may like to try the following experiment with your group. It is called 'the seagull'. This is an experiment in thought transference, and it demonstrates just how effective projecting one's thoughts can be.

First, ask the most psychically sensitive of the group to sit at the front, with their back to the others. They should sit in a relaxed position, with their eyes closed, endeavouring to attune their thoughts to everyone in the room.

Hand out to each of the group (but not to the person at the front) small, folded pieces of paper, upon which you have written a word. Tell members of the group that every word is different, and that they must not allow anyone else to see what their particular word is. Explain to them that they are going to transmit these words to the person at the front, and that part of the experiment's success depends on this secrecy.

In fact, every piece of paper will contain the same word, i.e. *SEAGULL.*

When everyone is seated, relaxed and ready to begin, ask the group to close their eyes, and to sit for a few moments focused on their word, establishing it clearly in the mind. Tell them that they must now imagine a thin beam of golden light, passing from their forehead to the back of the person at the front. Once it is established, so that they can see this beam of light very clearly in the mind, and they have become totally aware of the force behind it, they can then allow the beam to gradually fade.

Now group members can begin to transmit their word, either as a picture which they have created in their mind, or simply as the word is written. The group member at the front must allow their mind to remain passive, and yet they should be aware of any thoughts, feelings or impressions which they may experience, calling these out clearly to the group. Should anyone hear their word thus given, they should respond immediately. It is a good idea for the experiment supervisor to make a note of *everything* that is called out by the person to whom the words are being directed. It can take time for the group to develop a rapport among themselves, and most of the things called out initially may be only loosely connected to 'the word'. For example, a picture of a cloud might be received. These may have been transmitted by one of the group along with the picture of a seagull. The sun shining on the horizon may also be received but, again, the seagull may not. The person who is projecting the word often projects the whole scene which they have created around it. So, until the one receiving the pictures has developed the ability to notice detail, only fragments of the whole picture will be received.

However, spectacular results can occur quite spontaneously in this experiment, and would, therefore, demonstrate the remarkable telepathic abilities possessed by both those transmitting and by the one who is receiving. This method is in no way a test of the psychic abilities of those taking part. It is more an exercise to aid the development of telepathic powers. Of course, once those participating in the experiment realize that the same word has been given to everyone, it cannot be practised in the same way again. From then on different words can be given to the group.

The exercise can prove to be a powerful aid to the training and development of the powers of the mind, and it clearly demonstrates, to all who witness it, just what great potential lies within us all. The experiment demonstrates just how effective our collective forces can be, when focused on one target. In fact, when developing your psychic powers you must not underestimate your own abilities, nor the things you have yet to achieve. There is no such word as *impossible* where the sciences of the mind are concerned, and it is only by continuous experimentation that you will come to develop and discover the real psychic you.

The creative aspects of the mind often assimilate the information received from the outward world into ideas of shapes and colours, which then, being symbollically presented to us through the mechanism of the mind, our consciousness immediately places in some understandable order.

Working with different coloured shapes helps to cultivate the imagery faculty and aids the development of our mental powers. The conditioning to which we have been subjected throughout our lives limits our perception and range of awareness, preventing us from looking, listening and feeling beyond the field of our five normal senses.

When we look at an object we normally see the front of the object alone, as a single dimension, never the front, back and the sides collectively, which together constitute the whole. So, looking at it in this way, we can see how limited our perception of the world in which we live really is.

However, our mind does not have the same limitations of awareness as for example, our eyes. What our eyes are unable to perceive, our mind certainly can. By training the mind along specific lines, we may develop the ability to direct the consciousness beyond any boundaries. The ability to almost 'look through' solid objects is not as crazy as it may sound, because training the mind to penetrate matter is part and parcel of being psychic.

Again, I would say that when endeavouring to develop such powers, the imagination must be allowed free rein and total freedom. Allowing yourself to 'let go' completely is of paramount importance. Imposing limitations upon yourself merely restricts your psychic development.

Exercise 20

For this exercise you will need a generous quantity of small envelopes, and as many different coloured shapes as possible. They can be made from card bought from any good stationers. Use squares, circles, stars, oblongs, ovals, triangles, and any other shapes you can think of.

First of all, place one shape in each envelope and mix all the envelopes together in a box or bag. Then distribute them among the members of the group. Divide the group into pairs.

As your partner holds up each envelope in turn, endeavour to determine which shapes and colours are contained within, without actually touching the envelopes yourself. Keep a record of your successes.

The technique used in this particular exercise is quite simple, but it takes time and effort to develop. Instead of just staring at the envelope, you should actually gaze 'through' it, almost like staring into space, as though you are day-dreaming. Look right 'through' the envelope, as though it is not there. Ignore it completely. If you can resist the temptation to blink, all the better; if not, simply hold your gaze for as long as possible before blinking, then slowly close your eyes.

Although the after image of the envelope itself will eventually appear in your mind's eye, other more nebulous images will also be seen. These, however, will be very fleeting, and will appear to come and go as quickly as the blink of an eye. It is important to respond immediately to the first image you see, and not to analyse what you think you may have seen.

The colour is usually the first thing to appear, and is very often much clearer than the shape. The two may not appear together, so the shape may appear colourless. This is why you must train your mind to watch very carefully. It is simply a case of practising and of knowing exactly what to look for, because the images and impressions you receive may not be in any particular order.

Do not be put off by the simplicity of this exercise nor, for that matter, by your personal views and opinions. In other words, try to think beyond all that you can see, beyond all that you can hear, and beyond all that you can feel. Try not to allow yourself to become disheartened or discouraged by the lack of immediate successful results.

 Exercise 21

This exercise has many possibilities, and you certainly do not have to restrict yourself to coloured shapes.

Ask your partner to stand behind a screen, or even to move into an adjacent room, and to hold an object (unknown to you) in their hands. Using the same process as in Exercise 20, try to gaze 'through' the wall, ignoring it completely, and resisting the temptation to blink. The most difficult part of this exercise is trying to ignore whatever obstructs your vision. However, once you have learned to 'block out', you will find that it is just as easy to ignore a wall as it is an envelope in order to see whatever is obscured from your field of vision. Remember to continue the gazing process for as long as possible, then close your eyes to receive the imagery information. Remember: you are not looking with your eyes – you are using the imagery faculty, a sort of primitive 'homing' device which you have long since forgotten how to use, to obtain the information.

The other thing it is important to understand about this exercise is that we are not endeavouring to receive information telepathically from either the person, or the vibratory composition of the object. On the contrary, it is the aim of this exercise to actually 'see' the object with the mind's eye. This is, admittedly, a little more difficult, but once the technique has been mastered, looking through walls will appear just as easy to demonstrate as telepathically receiving information from another mind, without using the intermediary of the senses.

The development of the psychic faculties also amplifies information received via the five physical senses, whose range is somehow increased as a direct result. Although your short-sightedness will not improve as a result of your psychic abilities, your other four senses will certainly compensate for any impairment of your vision.

Considering this sort of sensory amplification, one must expect to be oversensitive at times and prone to mood swings, at least until your development is fully established, and your nervous system adjusts and settles down.

PSYCHIC HANDWRITING ANALYSIS

Some years ago I found I had an aptitude for picking things up psychically from people's handwriting. I would simply scan it very briefly, to glean all sorts of information about the person who had written it. Today I receive letters from all over the world requesting a psychic handwriting analysis.

Psychic handwriting analysis is quite different from graphology, which itself is a precise science, and involves an extensive and meticulous study of the structure and formation of the writing. Graphology offers limited information about the person's general character, skills and mood tendencies, and it certainly cannot reveal information pertaining to the writer's future.

Psychic handwriting analysis is different because the information is obtained through psychic means, and therefore the past, the present and the future become apparent to me, simply by quickly scanning the handwriting, or even holding it gently in my fingertips without looking at it.

Over the years I have found that some handwriting 'speaks' very clearly and loudly, and appears to want to tell all, while other handwriting appears shy and afraid, and almost reluctant to reveal information. This is the only way I am able to describe psychic handwriting analysis, because the information gleaned from it varies from person to person.

While this method cannot exactly be taught, I *can* offer you some pointers and general guidelines as to how you can make psychic handwriting analysis work for you.

Exercise 22

First, ask the group to obtain some samples of handwriting from people whom they know quite well. This will allow any information given during the exercise to be confirmed. Distribute the handwriting samples to the group. Obviously, make sure they all receive writing unknown to them.

Sit quietly with the sample of writing. Allow your eyes to scan it continuously backwards and forwards. Impressions should come to you almost immediately, and as with the psychometry exercise (Exercise 9), write them down straight away.

First, get a general feeling for the person's character and emotional status. Are they happy? Are they alone in life? What sort of career do they have? Are they creative? Divorced? Widowed?

It is important to constantly ask yourself questions, jotting down the answers immediately. A lot of the information should come voluntarily, but the rest will need some persuasion.

Use all your senses during the exercise; smell the writing, feel it, listen to it and allow your eyes to constantly move across it. In other words, become totally involved with the writing and allow your mind to blend completely with it.

Obviously, check the accuracy of the information you obtain once you have completed the exercise.

It may be that psychic handwriting analysis is not your forte, and therefore will not work for you. Some people's sensitivity simply does not work along certain lines, and their particular skills need a different form of expression. Although it is a psychic ability, psychic handwriting analysis is not something that everyone can develop, and if it is going to work for you, it should work almost immediately. However, should psychic handwriting analysis prove to be something with which you feel quite comfortable, experiment with it as much as possible. Only with time and much practice will the skill be perfected. Remember: it is better if the writer's gender and age are unknown to you, because these things should become apparent to you once you have mastered this particular psychic skill.

Once your psychic abilities have been established, and they become more apparent to you, I would suggest that you use your group work as a means of experimenting with new ideas. Combining your ideas with those of the rest of the group can be quite constructive, and may even give rise to other psychic abilities which you never knew you possessed, such as, for example, receiving information from people who you know to be dead.

Latent mediumistic skills often develop as a result of group work, particularly in those people whose psychic powers have been there potentially from childhood, and have seemingly developed very quickly over the previous twelve months or so. In such cases that person needs special supervision and must not be encouraged to sit for development alone, particularly in the early stages of mediumistic development.

Thus a group is preferable if the mediumistic ability is something you are endeavouring to develop. While I would agree with the old saying 'Mediums are born', I believe that the ability can also be developed.

We will look more closely at this development in the next chapter.

chapter 6

MEDIUMSHIP AND TALKING WITH THE DEAD

BEFORE WE EXPLORE the endless possibilities of the wonderful gift of mediumship, we must first of all get our definitions right.

To begin with, not all mediums are clairvoyant, and not all clairvoyants are mediums and, therefore, able to 'see' the so called 'dead'. A medium is someone who is able to receive information from discarnates, either by seeing them, hearing them or merely sensing them.

The term 'clairvoyant' is applied to anyone who has the ability to see things which nobody else can, such as situations and events in the future or past. This sort of information is gleaned through a variety of methods of divination, ranging from tasseomancy (teacup reading) to crystal gazing and cartomancy (reading the cards).

A clairvoyant who possesses the ability to actually 'see' those whom we know to be dead also possesses mediumistic abilities. Although some clairvoyants are able to 'see' discarnate personalities, the absence of other psychic abilities simply makes the information they are able to receive from discarnates very limited.

Although the word 'clairvoyance' is the one most people are familiar with (it literally means 'clear seeing'), other mediumistic abilities include 'clairaudience' (clear hearing) and 'clairsentience' (clear sensing).

It may come as a surprise to some to learn that, simply by 'sensing' a spirit presence, a medium is quite often able to describe everything about that person, from the colour of their eyes and hair to their height and the cause of their death. The gift of clairsentience can be so uncannily accurate that to onlookers it often appears as though the medium is actually seeing, hearing and holding a conversation with the spirit of the dead person. However, this is certainly not the case.

The gift of clairaudience, or the ability to hear the voices of the dead, is quite rare. However, many clairsentient mediums mistakenly believe that they are receiving their information clairaudiently, simply because their gift of clairsentience can be so clear that it sometimes seems as if a voice is speaking to them.

Although clairaudience involves the auditory faculties controlling the sense of hearing, the spirit voices are not always that clear, and they can manifest in different ways. Sometimes a spirit voice can appear as a muffled sound, almost as though someone is speaking to you from an adjacent room. At other times it resembles a clear voice audible from the side of you. Sometimes, however, clairaudient voices appear as no more than extraneous thoughts, passing quickly through the brain.

One of the most common misconceptions concerning mediumship is that a medium has the power to 'call' the discarnate back and to command communication with them. No matter who, or how powerful, the medium happens to be, it is simply not possible to command spirit communication. A medium acts as an intermediary between two worlds, a sort of telephone exchange, or even a radio which has to be tuned in to the correct wavelength. If the spirit world decides not to communicate for any reason there is nothing that can be done. For this reason alone, mediumistic communications must always be considered as purely experimental, because the results cannot in any way be guaranteed.

Although most mediums have possessed their abilities from early childhood, it *is* something that can be developed. However, one cannot pick and choose which ability one wants to develop, as the choice is not ours to make. One's psychic powers are merely developed and refined with practice. Thus you should neither compare yourself to other psychics nor envy the way in which they work.

Development takes place in the faculty corresponding to the chakra in which the ability is already potentially present. By the use of specific methods, the inherent powers are encouraged and thus released. While mediumship takes many forms, it is with the aspects of mediumistic abilities which come under the label of 'mental mediumship' that we shall be concerned in this book. The other form of mediumship, that termed 'physical mediumship', is far too extensive a subject to cover in one chapter. As I am more concerned with the spontaneity of psychic development, we will confine ourselves to what is, I feel, the very interesting subject of mental mediumship.

Let us look once again at the various forms of mental mediumship and their exact definitions.

Clairvoyance: The ability to 'see' clearly those things which are beyond the normal visible spectrum.

Clairaudience: The gift of 'hearing' clearly sounds which are outside and beyond the normal range of hearing.

Clairsentience: The ability to 'sense' the subtle vibratory atmosphere.

The traditional method for the development of mediumistic powers is to sit in a *development circle*, usually under the supervision of a competent teacher or medium.

Although this approach has always been extremely safe and reliable, and one in which some very famous and remarkably gifted mediums have developed their skills, I will only touch upon it briefly here, just enough to give you a good idea of what is involved when you 'sit' in a development circle.

A development circle is nearly always opened with a prayer, which acts as a sort of affirmation or declaration to the spirit world that the circle has begun. The supervising medium will often instruct those present to make their minds quiet by slow, rhythmic breathing, and to relax the body as completely as possible, while endeavouring to clear the mind of all mundane and anxious thoughts. A period of silence usually follows which may last for half an hour or more, during which time the participants are asked to make themselves receptive to the impulses of the spirit world.

After the period of silence, the instructing medium will ask each circle member to say what, if anything, they felt, and what impressed them during the silence.

This sort of development circle teaches the aspiring medium a great deal of discipline, and allows the spirit world to come close, to aid the 'sitters' in their endeavours. However, it is important that you feel comfortable with, and have total trust in, those with whom you work in the psychic field. As the psychic senses begin to develop and sharpen, so the physical senses become intensified. This profound and often dramatic transformation affects the emotions, making the person extremely sensitive and quite often insecure. It is therefore vitally important that a great deal of reassurance and encouragement be given to the student, particularly in the early stages of development.

Although the traditional development circle is a tried and tested method and one which has been used since Victorian times, it is my opinion that as the planet enters the zodiacal sign of Aquarius, and we move into the New Age, a whole new concept of spirit is beginning to manifest across the face of mankind. A great deal of interest is now being shown in all subjects of a metaphysical nature, and the methods of psychic development employed by those pioneers, in the early days are gradually being replaced with new and extremely exciting techniques. This is not in any way to decry the old methods, for they are the foundations upon which to build more modified techniques, better suited to the approaching twenty-first century.

Whatever mediumistic ability you may appear to be developing, meditation should form an integral part of your training programme in order that you can learn to focus the consciousness, thereby emptying the mind of all the useless garbage it has collected throughout the day. Combining a meditation programme with specific experimental exercises is most effective when endeavouring to encourage the development of clairvoyance.

When clairvoyance first begins to develop it is quite common to experience spontaneous psychic images, which always appear to happen so fast as to leave you thinking it was all in your imagination. Seeing lights moving around the bedroom before going to sleep, or even minute faces passing very quickly through your mind, are some of the typical experiences one has during the early stages of psychic development.

It is not uncommon to become transfixed as you look at intricate patterns on curtains or perhaps on a carpet, and to see these patterns appear to transform into the faces of unfamiliar people, or even animals. All these experiences are quite common as the faculties begin to quicken with psychic energy and the gift of clairvoyance-begins to unfold.

Using a gift before it develops fully can also be a useful form of encouragement, and in many cases this use strengthens the ability.

An experimental exercise which I have used in my workshops for quite some time, and which I call 'spontaneous mediumship', has helped to develop the abilities of some very good mediums.

 ## Exercise 23

All that is needed is a small invited audience, preferably comprised of people whose backgrounds are unknown to the developing medium.

This useful training exercise has two aims:

1. To develop the aspiring medium's style of presentation.

2. To encourage the clairvoyant ability.

First, introduce the aspiring medium to the audience. Then he or she will demonstrate their mediumistic skills by playing the role of a medium as though acting out a role in a play.

Standing in front of the audience, the aspiring medium should select someone from the group at random and proceed to give that person a 'message', as though the information is being received from someone who is dead. The medium must of course use his or her imagination to describe the features and physical stature of the 'dead' person whom they have created in their own mind. Without pausing to think about what they are saying they should continue to relate names and personal details, and to say anything and everything that comes into their mind.

The 'making up as you go along' approach is all part of the exercise, and it is only at the conclusion of the demonstration that the *accuracy* of the 'message' will become a reality, when it becomes clear just how much of the information is correct and has been confirmed.

Although the audience, and the aspiring medium, may feel as though the whole thing is just a charade, the use of the imagery faculties in this particular way somehow creates a subliminal bridge between the mind of the medium and the spirit world. It is across this bridge that 'connections' are spontaneously made and, during the developing medium's attempt to create a demonstration of genuine mediumship, true spirit communication filters into their consciousness.

I am not saying that every bit of information which is given in this way comes from a genuine source. However, I have seen it work successfully so many times that probably 80 per cent or more of the information given during such a demonstration will be accurately placed. Although the exercise resembles a party game, it is certainly one which can prove invaluable to an aspiring medium, and it is of course most effective in precipitating the gift of clairvoyance.

I have already said that the gift of clairaudience is rare, even though many mediums mistakenly believe that they possess it. It is one of those psychic abilities which has to be potentially present to enable it to be developed.

Although this is so with all psychic skills to some greater or lesser degree, clairaudience will not be encouraged to manifest unless the person has had *some* experience of it, and such experience usually originates from the medium's childhood. However, should you believe that you possess clairaudient abilities, but the experiences which you have had have been quite spasmodic and therefore not under your control, this ability *can* be 'amplified' by the following method.

Clairaudience has, more often than not, been present from childhood, and the chakra responsible for its manifestation also controls the vibratory impulses which cause everyday sound to manifest in the small space of the eardrum, causing that sense we term 'hearing'. Thus, by blocking out the vibratory manifestations of sound reaching our normal hearing, we can cause a quickening in the throat chakra in order to encourage its further activation.

Exercise 24

After a period of meditation and rhythmic breathing, sit quietly for a further five or ten minutes. Then, if possible, go out into your garden or a local park, or sit beside an open window.

Close your eyes and count exactly how many different sounds you can hear, such as birds singing, the rustle of leaves, the involuntary cracking of branches, the wind brushing the grass, and any other sounds your senses can pick up.

Listen to the sounds beyond the immediate, such as traffic, dogs barking, children playing, an aeroplane overhead, and so on. Be totally aware of your surroundings and beyond, and for a few moments endeavour to become totally attuned to nature. While attuning your thoughts and becoming relaxed, you will probably be able to pick out far away sounds that are almost inaudible to the physical ear.

Spend about half an hour on this part of the exercise. Then, still with eyes closed, plug your ears so as not to permit even the slightest sound to pass into the ear drum. It will probably take you a few minutes to adjust to the sudden deafness and the effect can be disorientating. However, something will seem to 'come alive' inside you – at least, that is the best way I can describe the sensation.

At this point you should try to become totally aware of the vastness of the space around you. The aim here is not to hear specific sounds, but more to develop an inner awareness, which will only be achieved when all other distractions have been excluded. It takes time to expand one's awareness in this way, but I have never known it to fail.

It may be that at the beginning of the exercise you will hear nothing at all. However, with a serious, determined approach to your psychic development, and with regular practice over a period of time, this exercise should gradually produce positive results. As with most skills, it is important to practise regularly, and although it may be neither practical nor realistic to do so every day, you really should try to find time to work at it at least three times a week in order to get a proper feeling for it.

Once the chakras have settled down to the fact that the senses are being withdrawn, as in the case of the hearing, there is usually a sudden quickening of energy in the throat and brow area to compensate for the withdrawal.

Remember: this exercise will only aid the development of the gift of clairaudience if it is already potentially present. In these cases it will help the aspirant to bring it more under their conscious control. The exercise can, however, help to precipitate a much deeper awareness of the senses, attuning them more acutely to the more sublime aspects of the Universe.

As with all mediumistic abilities, clairaudience is a gift of the spirit, and should therefore be treated as such. As it develops it should be encouraged, and this can be achieved by laying strong foundations of knowledge and spiritual awareness. Once the great door of the faculties has been opened to the world of the discarnate, those who approach you may not always be of the kind that you would choose to call. The vagabonds, the rogues, the villains and the debauched of *this* world become themselves, and more so, in the next world.

Discipline and caution make a wise man strong, and where psychic development is concerned you are only as strong as your weakest attribute. It is certainly not the angelic forces alone who seek to help you in your spiritual endeavours, but as you become a vessel of light, as all mediums must be, those vagabonds of the lower astral world, whose sole intention it is to prevent such light from manifesting in this world, seek to gravitate towards you. A medium's path is certainly not an easy one, and one needs, for one's own protection, to develop inner strength and to cultivate the habit of thinking higher and more spiritual thoughts.

There are other skills which come under the umbrella of mental mediumship, and which can also be developed. These are as follows:

Psychic Art

The ability to sketch a portrait of a 'dead' person whose presence has either been 'felt', or whose form has been 'seen' by the artist. Should you be in the slightest way artistic, you may consider combining your psychic abilities with your artistic skills, and using them in this way.

Psychic art is a very visual way of working, and can be extremely evidential when endeavouring to offer proof of someone's continued existence after death. This is, after all, the primary object of mediumship. The same method of spontaneous mediumship can be used successfully to aid the development of psychic art.

Most of the psychic artists I have known claim to have no clairvoyant skills, and therefore to 'see' nothing at all. One can thus only assume that their ability to sketch an accurate portrait of a 'dead' person rests purely upon intuitive means. Demonstrating their artistic skills in the spontaneous mediumship exercise will produce the same, if not better results.

 ## Exercise 25

The aspiring psychic artist should sit or stand in front of the audience, sketch pad and pencil at the ready. Once again, select a member of the audience at random as the subject.

The psychic artist can initiate an accurate demonstration of psychic art by simply allowing his or her pencil to intuitively create the first image (of a person) that comes into his or her mind. He or she should add a little verbal information to the sketch, and the recipient will very probably be able to place or recognize the person in the drawing.

These experiments make the sometimes boring aspects of development a little more interesting. However, they are also of prime importance in helping to promote in the aspiring medium a more professional presentation and interesting style of working.

Spirit Writing

Often termed 'automatic writing', this is the ability to receive written messages from discarnate souls, which are always outside the conscious control of the writer. In fact the writings are involuntary, and can even be written when the medium's mind is occupied elsewhere. They usually appear in a script quite different to that of the writer's normal hand. The writings often happen so quickly that all the words are joined together, and move from one passage to another with no punctuation.

Inspirational Writing

This is often confused with automatic writing, but it is completely different. Although a lesser and more common form of mediumship, it is certainly one which should not be disregarded.

With this form of writing the writer feels 'inspired' by discarnate minds, who appear to use the mind of the writer to express their own philosophical thoughts, views and ideas. During the writing process the medium is totally conscious of what is being written, unlike the automatic writer who is not.

Most, if not all, poets, writers, musicians and even artists have claimed at some time to have been inspired by some supernatural force. Some have even said that without experiencing this force they find it useless to even attempt to write or create anything.

It was Lord Byron who said, 'Poetry is a distinct faculty – it won't come when called – you may as well whistle for the wind.' I am quite sure that he was speaking of inspiration.

I have known writing mediums to describe that feeling which overwhelms them, when they are inspired to write something, as being akin to some immense power flooding their very being. For me, inspiration causes a quickening of all my senses. I feel totally preoccupied with the theme of what I am writing, so much so that my heart quickens and my senses become totally oblivious to anyone or anything around me. When I have finished writing it often seems as though some force is lifted from me, leaving me with a strange sense of emotion.

Inspirational writing is not, as I have already said, to be confused with automatic writing, which is completely involuntary. The only feature which inspirational writing and automatic writing have in common is that the writings which are produced most certainly come from a metaphysical source, over which no control can in any way be exercised.

I rarely have the least idea of what I am going to write about before I sit down at my desk. But then I suddenly feel overwhelmed with specific feelings which I can usually relate to certain discarnate personalities whom I have come to know, and with whom I have developed a strong relationship over the years. These feelings often mean that a specific theme will be followed in the writings.

The approach to the development of inspirational writing must be the same as the approach to the development of automatic writing. It may well be that you have for a long time felt the presence, or even the closeness of a spirit personality which, for some reason, has compelled you to pick up your pen.

Quite often to begin with, nothing very spectacular happens with either of these abilities. In the case of inspirational writing one is inclined to sit there searching the mind for appropriate thoughts to put down, but these often drop into the consciousness without the control of the writer, and can flood the mind with images, feelings and ideas.

Automatic writing also needs a totally quiet mind, but the attention of the writer should be directed elsewhere other than to the pen and paper.

 ## Exercise 26

Once you feel sure that this is the medium through which you are going to work, it is often advisable to loosely hold a pencil over a piece of paper and, in the other hand, a book which interests you – preferably one which is completely unrelated to psychic matters.

Read the book, allowing it to engross you. Try to forget the pencil in your other hand. At first, do not sit for longer than half an hour. The duration may be increased as you become more confident. Remember to send out your thoughts beforehand, expressing your strong and serious desire to be 'used' in this way.

If, after practising in this way for a few months, nothing has happened (bearing in mind that this ability can take a long time to develop), it might be a good idea to obtain a planchette to encourage the technique along a little. A planchette is a small ball or wheel in which a pencil is placed. It can move around with greater ease than can the hand.

It is better to 'sit' at the same time every evening, and you must be punctual each time you sit. As the concept of time in the spirit world is completely different to that which we know, there being no alternating periods of night and day, it is of great benefit to your discarnate 'helpers' to be guided by your punctuality. This will also reassure them of your dedication and seriousness to the task.

Trance Mediumship

This mediumistic ability has various levels, ranging from a slight 'overshadowing', in which the medium is still conscious and aware of their surroundings, and very often also aware of what is being said, to deep trance, in which the medium is completely unconscious of what is being said.

With the latter ability the medium appears to fall into a light sleep, awakening with a different persona, often speaking with a different accent, and, on rare occasions, able to speak a foreign language which is completely unknown to the medium. Trance mediumship is an ability which must be developed under the supervision of someone who is knowledgeable on the subject, and who is sufficiently qualified to take care of the developing medium should any problems be encountered during the trance state.

I am referring here to difficulties concerning the medium's revival from the trance state which can unfortunately sometimes occur.

The principal problem with deeply controlled trance is that the medium retains no knowledge of what is said during trance, and therefore nothing is ever learned (by the medium) from any philosophical discourses given by the spirit control.

If you sit in a group for the development of mediumship, and you are showing some trance potential, you will experience different states of awareness during meditative exercises. You will often experience unusual feelings such as overwhelming sensations of buoyancy, and an inability to decide whether you are sitting upright, horizontally or upside down. You may also experience feelings of moving quickly down a dark tunnel, towards a bright light at the end of it. This can be very unnerving to the developing medium. One can therefore understand why it is so important that a high standard of supervision be provided, particularly in the early stages of psychic development.

Incidentally, all these experiences usually appear to take place within the space of a few minutes. It is no great surprise, therefore, to discover, when the meditation is over, that a full hour has often passed by. You may even be told that during this time you rose to your feet and spoke with a strange voice – that of a disembodied personality.

Should the development of trance mediumship be your main interest, your approach to it should be more or less the same as your approach to the development of mental mediumistic abilities. That is, some knowledge should first of all be acquired as to the fundamental rudiments of meditation and rhythmic breathing. Although this approach is not specifically the traditional one, it is certainly the one which I would advocate for anyone embarking upon the path of psychic development.

The primary object of the following exercise is to promote total stillness of the mind. Allow the consciousness to be focused completely upon that stillness.

 Exercise 27

Previously (p. 48), I talked about counting your pulse beats to use as an accompaniment to your measured breathing. This will give you the rhythm to the count of six – three – six, and so on. When you have mastered this technique move to the next step.

Sit in an easy, relaxed position, shoulders back, hands resting lightly in your lap, your eyes closed. Ascertain your pulse beats by counting with them from 1 to 12, 1 to 12, 1 to 12, and so on. Breathe in to the (mental) accompaniment of 1,2,3,4,5,6,7,8,9,10,11,12. Hold your breath for the count of six; breathe out to the count of 12; hold it for the count of three, and so on.

When you can breathe almost unconsciously in this way, focus totally upon the flow of air coming into your body. Control it very carefully as it moves into the lungs and then into the nervous system. This technique of breathing brings about a greater sense of awareness, making the psyche more receptive to psychic impulses.

I would suggest that this technique be followed regularly, regardless of whether or not you are using it as a prelude to entering a meditative state.

It is of paramount importance, when endeavouring to develop trance mediumship, to sit with those whom you can trust.

The various levels of consciousness through which you will eventually pass to attain a state of control, and being controlled, need to be monitored very carefully. There must always be a cautionary note about this sort of development. While in even a semi-trance state you are quite often putting your safe-keeping into the hands of those around you, both seen and unseen. One, therefore, needs to be extremely disciplined, with a strong mind, during development of this kind. Any feelings of apprehension should be carefully noted, for these may represent the finger of caution.

Be assured of one thing, however: if you take time with your development, and are meticulous in the way you formulate your training programme, you will certainly be pleased with the end results.

Once a clairvoyant ability begins to develop, there is always a temptation for the developing medium to be influenced in some way by the facial expressions of the person to whom they are giving a 'message'. Sometimes they may unconsciously give a general character reading, thinking that the information they are receiving is being psychically obtained, when, in fact, it is not.

A developing medium must overcome feelings of self-consciousness and lack of confidence, and they would certainly be forgiven for being put off, by the sometimes critical or doubting looks on the faces of the recipients of their messages.

The expressions on the faces of members of an audience can be very off-putting, even to the most competent and experienced of mediums. One may, in fact, find that an audience has created an atmosphere not at all conducive for a successful demonstration of mediumship to take place.

A common misconception, subscribed to by many mediums, is that they must hear the voice of the person to whom they are giving a 'message'. It is their belief that this strengthens the link with the spirit communicator, and without it they fear that the link may be broken. This is a complete fallacy, and invariably the result of poor training and lack of confidence in their ability. If a mediumistic demonstration is going to work, it will work, regardless of whether or not the medium is able to hear any response from the person to whom they are speaking, or, for that matter, whether or not they can see them.

I once had the privilege of knowing an elderly medium who was both deaf and visually handicapped, and had been so since birth. This man never failed to amaze me with the accuracy of his messages. He would simply point a finger at the person to whom he wanted to speak, and give the message.

This point, that of whether or not the medium needs to hear the respondent's voice, may be illustrated more fully by a simple exercise.

 ## Exercise 28

The aspiring medium should give their demonstration in much the same way as they did the spontaneous mediumship exercise (Exercise 23), but this time they should wear a blindfold.

Instead of giving an audible response, the audience member to whom the medium is speaking will simply nod or shake their head. The supervising teacher will take the part of intermediary, and will audibly pass on the response to the medium. There will, therefore, be no audible contact between medium and recipient.

This exercise may not work immediately, and the medium may find him- or herself struggling to give accurate information, but only because, without the use of the senses of hearing and sight, the aspiring medium will probably lack confidence. However, once this initial problem is overcome they should be amazed at the results.

chapter 7

CHANNELLING THE POWERS OF THE MIND

MOST PEOPLE LIVE out their lives from day to day, completely unaware of the powers which lie within them. A working person often experiences the day's routine almost mechanically, having gone through the same things day in, day out, for years. Regardless of whether they are more or less content or completely dissatisfied with their lives, the majority of people are ignorant of the fact that there are such powers within their minds which, if channelled and released, could transform both themselves and their lives completely.

The poor man only dreams of being wealthy, thinking that riches are far beyond his reach. The weak and sickly person wishes for good health and strength, and the unhappy person hopes and prays for happiness. Most people live lives of hopes, wishes and dreams, without possessing the knowledge that they could be in control of an inner power that is far greater than all these things.

It is easy to understand why anyone would find it difficult to think in a positive way when they encounter one problem after another, pushing them further and further into a state of despair. It is all very well to be told 'Be positive!', but when you lack confidence you are consequently unable to think positively about your life. A person lacking in confidence and motivation has probably spent a lifetime creating the fragile foundations upon which his or her life is built;

thus transforming a life that is uncertain and weak into one which is positive and strong seems a near impossibility.

Once a person's negative habits have been allowed to internally crystallize, they will gradually solidify into external situations and circumstances. Changing the habits of a lifetime is extremely difficult, but certainly not impossible.

When you are worried or anxious about something which is generally impairing the quality of your life, you probably find some comfort in sitting and relaxing for a few moments, quietly turning the problem over in your mind, and exploring all the ways in which your predicament might be resolved. But more often than not, somewhere along the line, the imagination takes control, creating emotions which eventually convince you that things are definitely going to get worse. There is far more truth in the old saying, 'You will worry yourself into an early grave' than you might imagine. It therefore makes sense that if you are able to worry yourself into the grave, the same principles must apply to thinking your way to good health, success and happiness.

I mentioned above that 'thoughts are living things', and that we are all pulled along by the thoughts and desires which we have previously set in motion. However, when struggling in the mire of self-created despair and panic, the only way to free yourself from such negative conditions is to allow yourself to develop the realization that these dark emotions have no real connection with your problems other than the connection you yourself make with them.

Worrying about situations and events that have not yet happened quite often hastens their approach, and makes the thinker vulnerable and more susceptible to other, similar situations and events.

The way forward is to create new images in the imagination and to set these free, rather like large, helium-filled balloons floating off into space. You must create more than one image – don't forget that you have probably taken a lifetime to flood your life with worry and despair, so the first move forward must be with the positive realization that within you there exists the power that can now set you free.

Those of you who have made a study of meditation, and explored the possibilities of mind power, will know that the electrical impulses produced by the brain change somewhat when certain meditative states are reached. These electrical impulses can be measured by connecting the meditator to an electroencephalograph (EEG) which measures and records the cyclic changes of electricity which occur in the brain during meditation. This offers us conclusive evidence that meditation is capable of producing measurable changes in the brain.

A deep meditative state is often referred to as the 'alpha state', the term used to designate the brainwave patterns produced by meditation. This state also has a much wider effect upon the physiological make-up of the person.

The alpha state is also reached during sleep – when totally relaxed, or even when day-dreaming. However, as there are often different levels to one's sleep patterns, the electrical energies produced by the brain also vary, and move from alpha to theta and to delta. Being fully awake and getting on with life's daily chores is performed while the brain is in beta, in which state numerous different feelings are experienced, depending entirely upon how the day is going for us.

The positive transformation of one's life must first of all begin with the certain knowledge that *you do possess the power to transform it*. Such a transformation involves the process of burning out the negative images which furnish your life, and which you have created over a lifetime of wrong thinking, and the creation of new and more positive images, giving them enough energy to sustain them.

 ## Exercise 29

Try to relax totally, either sitting in a comfortable chair or lying on the bed. Close your eyes and 'see' your life as it presently is, full of worries, problems and anxieties. For a few moments allow yourself to relive each of these negative mental states. Allow your mind to go over all the things which present a problem for you, and create a grey balloon around each one.

Continue this process, until you have a clear picture in your imagination of yourself clutching the strings to which the grey balloons are attached. In your imagination, see yourself in control of the balloons, and when you are quite ready, release them with a smile. As they float off into the air, again using the power of your imagination, will them to return to you and, as they do so, once again take hold of the strings.

Hold the balloons for a moment, reaffirming what is contained within them, and once again using your imagination, check that each balloon still represents each of your problems.

Release them again, and watch them float off into the air. Allow them to move a little further away than before, then again draw them back towards you and, when they are close enough, reach out and take hold of the strings. Continue this process for as long as it takes for you to feel comfortable with the exercise. When you feel confident that you fully understand its object, and have begun to feel as though your problems are mentally under control, you can consider the next phase.

Although the cause of your worry and despair is objective, the actual feelings themselves are created subjectively. It is therefore at a subliminal level that the work must take place.

Seeing the balloons very clearly in your imagination, reach out and burst each one, allowing a moment to elapse between each impact. Be mindful of the fact that with the destruction of the balloons goes your worry and despair. Sit for a few moments relaxing before considering the next phase.

I am not suggesting for one moment that this exercise of the imagination will magically eradicate your financial difficulties, health problems, or any other seemingly insurmountable obstacle that you may be encountering in your everyday life, nor am I suggesting that you ignore these problems completely. On the contrary, life is difficult enough without adding complications. However, by learning to master the immense powers within you, you may exert a more positive control over your life, enabling you to become the master. Such a dramatic transformation of self has a much wider effect, not only on your mental life, but also on your physical and spiritual lives. Moving on to the next phase, allow your body to relax even more by breathing slowly and deeply, taking even breaths. Clear your mind completely. Feel yourself sinking almost into a state of sleep, totally relaxed and overwhelmed with a beautiful sense of peace and calm. When you feel relaxed enough, allow your imagination to light up the screen in your mind.

Now, focus totally on those things which you desire, such as prosperity, health, happiness and peace of mind. Place each in order of its importance to you. Create a brightly lit white balloon around each, and once again take hold of the strings to which they are attached. Allow your imagination to focus on each balloon, and what that balloon represents. See the balloons glowing in your imagination, gleaming brightly as they float in front of you. Look into each of the balloons and see the things you desire written very clearly in brightly glowing words. Then, as you did with the grey balloons, release them, allowing them to float upward. Watch them move away from you; then, using the strength and powers of your imagination once again, watch them being slowly drawn back towards you. When they are close enough, reach out, take hold of the strings and pull them nearer to you. Once again check the contents of each one, and make them glow even more brightly.

Repeat this process over and over again, until you feel confident that you have them all under your control. Should you still be unsure of the measure of your control over the balloons and what they represent, leave the exercise, and come back to it another time.

When you fully understand the object of the exercise, and you feel confident about your control over the balloons, consider all the balloons and the feelings, desires and emotions they represent, and create a word which collectively encapsulates them. The word can be anything, and take any form you like, as long as it is a word which you understand fully.

Once you have created your word, focus on it for as long as it takes to familiarize yourself completely with it. Remember that you have created this word and therefore understand the power behind it. Explore the word fully, occasionally allowing your thoughts to reconsider the things which the word represents for you. When you have total confidence in this word, and what is contained within it, allow your imagination to return to the white balloons. See them clearly in front of you and, one by one, destroy them, dissolving them completely from the screen in your imagination.

Move on to the next phase. Again, relax your body as deeply as you possibly can, clearing all residual images from your mind, and allowing yourself to drift once again to the point of sleep. Say to yourself, 'I will not sleep, I will only allow myself to be as totally relaxed as I possibly can.' Repeat this, breathing in and out slowly and deeply.

Once you have found a feeling of serenity, allow your imagination to light up the screen in your mind once again. Place your chosen word on the screen so that you can see it clearly. You are now going to convert that word into three separate finger positions which, when executed, will enable you to instantly release the inherent forces of your original desires.

First, familiarize yourself with the three separate movements which represent three different levels of achievement:

Movement one: Place your index finger between your brows for a brief moment. This movement will enable you to be assertive, confident and able to cope in any difficult situation.

The movement of the index finger to the space between the brows increases your capacity to concentrate and to project your personal magnetism, thereby affording you the confidence you require when under pressure. Interviews, starting a new career, exams, beginning new ventures, going it alone in business, using your powers of observation, solving problems, thinking things through; in other words, anything which requires you to be alert and attentive, may be achieved with the movement of the index finger to the brow.

This finger movement has a subliminal psychological effect upon the brow centre – *Ajna* – and will precipitate all the qualities required which have been created in the mental exercise.

Movement two: Touch the tip of your nose briefly with the middle finger of your right hand to release your deeper magnetic powers, so enabling you to overcome financial problems, and to gain a greater and more positive control over your financial life. By touching the tip of your nose you can overcome loneliness and feelings of insecurity, increasing your powers to attract new friends, good health, wealth, and a greater sense of adventure. This finger position also helps you to become more patient, astute and meticulous, and will also release those inner magnetic powers, affording you the 'Midas touch' in all that you do.

Once the technique has been fully mastered, this finger position helps to activate the channels of energy between the throat centre – *Vishudda* – and the brow centre – *Ajna* – affording you a greater and more powerful force of attraction.

The only cautionary note I would sound here is that this finger position must not be used for selfish means, or to hurt others, because this may cause the opposite effect to be experienced, reintroducing all the original negative situations and emotions with a force far greater than before.

Movement three: Touch your throat briefly with the little finger of your right hand to release a surge of psychic power, allowing you to see things much more clearly.

This finger movement will make you more intuitive, and will also aid the self-healing process of those recovering from illness. It will precipitate creative and psychic abilities, making them stronger and more dynamic. It helps to cultivate oratory abilities, making you more communicative and more able to convey your thoughts and feelings to others with far greater confidence.

This finger position releases the inherent powers of the throat centre – *Vishudda* – and affects your whole awareness and perception of objects, situations and people. It can also be of assistance when you are struggling to diet.

The finger positions themselves will have no effect at all unless the accompanying visualization exercise has been followed and practised regularly. To enable them to really work for you a programme has to be created first.

It is a good idea to make a list of all the things you would like to change in your life and all the things you want to achieve before attempting the exercise.

Although the exercise in creative visualization is important in making the finger positions work for you, try not to make it too complicated for yourself. Keep the quantity of balloons in the exercise to a minimum; you may even allow each balloon to contain more than one thing.

You will also find it of value to the results and effectiveness of the finger positions if you associate each balloon with one of them. For example, one or two balloons may contain a desire for wealth and happiness; in that case focus on the appropriate balloons for a few moments, then apply the finger to the corresponding position, thereby setting the programme in motion.

It may be the case that you find it easier to modify the exercise in some way, in order to suit your own grasp and understanding of it. This will not adversely affect the results, as long as the creative imagery exercise has been practised until the programme has been fully established in your mind. Remember, it does take time and practice to make the exercise work for you, but you can rest assured that your perseverance and determination will produce positive rewards.

Even when the technique has been fully mastered it is a good idea to practise it as regularly as possible, in order to reintroduce the imagery into the subconscious and to revitalize it with more power.

It may also be that you want to reprogramme the exercise occasionally, having achieved your previous aims. I would certainly suggest that you do this, as your abilities will benefit from an occasional 'clear out', just as though you were discarding an old and worn video tape and replacing it with a new and much clearer one.

chapter 8

PSYCHIC SELF-DEFENCE

E ARE CONSTANTLY being bombarded and influenced by the streams and waves of thoughts which have been set in motion by minds past and present, and we are often overwhelmed by the forces of such thoughts, to the extent of being pulled into the mire of depression or even encouraged to heights of grater fulfilment.

I am talking about those subtle atmospheres we all experience from time to time in old buildings, or even in specific geographical areas. However, some people are more sensitive to these vibratory atmospheres than others. None the less, regardless of whether or not one is sensitive, everyone is ultimately affected by the invisible forces that permeate the astral space surrounding them, and which often have the profound effect of flooding the mind with the emotions with which they were first created.

Although most psychic forces which are released into the atmosphere have no particular power behind them, and were perhaps not originally created with the intention of influencing the minds of other people, there are certain individuals who *do* create such forces with the sole intention of influencing others for either good or ill.

It is of paramount importance that those working in the psychic field should always be mindful of the fact that they, more than anyone else, are susceptible to psychic invasion either from incarnate minds, that is, others working in the same field who are aware of the powers they possess, or perhaps from discarnate vagabonds roaming menacingly through the lower vibratory spaces of the astral world.

No matter what the source of the invasion, the techniques of protection must ultimately be the same, and measures must therefore be taken immediately to create some form of positive protection. Continuous psychic attack can eventually wear down the psychic's levels of resistance to such a degree as to be extremely detrimental to their health. By infiltrating the psychic's aura, the invading thought forces gradually break down the energies of the mind, making it possible for the attacker to influence the psychic against his or her will.

Waiting for such an attack to take place before creating the protection is like closing the gate after the horse has bolted. I would suggest that you always work on the premise that a psychic attack is going to take place, and formulate a protective programme as soon as you even consider embarking upon metaphysical studies.

Furthermore, it is not always when you are awake that an attack may take place. Indeed, most 'psychic invasions' come when one is asleep. In this way the invading forces meet you on their own ground, in the lower regions of the astral world, where their malevolence is most powerful and able to exercise the greatest force.

Such attacks can be detrimental to the psychological make-up, and although the techniques of protection are more or less the same, the approach is slightly different inasmuch as specific thought forms need to be created with a particular mission in mind.

Whatever area of the psychic field you work in, a healthy and well-balanced approach is of great importance. There is no place for fanciful notions such as thinking that because your intentions are good and honourable you will automatically be afforded divine protection. Nor is there any place for ignorance and the belief that just because you do not know about it, harm will not come to you.

A great deal of nonsense is talked about psychic self-defence, and about what one ought and not ought to do. It is true that we are looked upon and guided to some extent by angelic forces, but it must also be understood that they are only as strong and as powerful as *your* weakest point, and they may even guide you into difficult situations whereby you can attain greater knowledge and experience.

While you sleep, and the physical senses are more or less anaesthetized to feeling, the consciousness functions in the astral body, and it is through this body's corresponding senses that knowledge and information is obtained about the astral world.

Most people do not have any recollection of their sojourn in the astral sleep state, but those who do remember find that the experiences they have mostly filter through into the conscious mind after having been transmuted into the symbolization of dreams. However, it would be ridiculous to suppose that all dreams represent the symbolic results of astral experiences, as the majority of our dreams are merely the results of over-indulgence of one kind or another, or even the mind's natural process of dealing with stress and anxiety. A recurring dream, however, is definitely the result of an astral experience, and may fit into one of two categories. The first is of a prophetic nature, and is usually termed a 'precognitive dream'. This is a dream from which prophetic information is gleaned, and which usually comes true in time. The second type of dream often reveals the dreamer in some dangerous situation, or even being killed. It is also quite common in this sort of dream for the dreamer to see him or herself as being dead. A dream of this nature is almost certainly the result of some sort of psychic attack, and it will certainly continue to recur until something is done about it.

A recurring dream featuring an assault upon the dreamer by some form of demon often means that malevolent forces have been set against them. In order to deal with this unfortunate case a specific thought form needs to be created over a period of time. This should then be released into the astral space each night before going into sleep.

The following process will help:

 # Psychic self-defence: Method one

Each night before going to sleep, lie quietly on your bed with your eyes fixed on a certain spot on the ceiling. Begin to breathe rhythmically, slowly and deeply, with even exhalations and inhalations. Resist the temptation to blink, but when the eyes move out of focus, slowly close them. Feel overwhelmed with a sense of peace. Create in your mind a beautiful pool of pulsating blue light, the kind of blue that colours a clear sky on a summer's day. Let this pool of blue light be full of movement, almost alive. See it very clearly in your mind. Imagine it almost filling your bedroom, surrounding you.

Across the surface of this pool create a golden equidistant cross, whose intersecting lines establish four points of contact at the circumference of the pool of blue light. In this way your sacred pool is sealed by the power of the equidistant cross. See yourself lying in the centre of this pool and allow the blue light to surround you. Now physically extend your arms, and imagine yourself lying on the cross. Feel the golden rays emanating from it and passing through you. Do not permit your mind to wander even for a moment from this picture of yourself and the pool.

Feel yourself becoming submerged in the pulsating pool of blue light, and mentally say to yourself five times: 'This is the sacred pool and I am filled with the power of the golden cross. No harm shall come to me.'

Re-create the sacred pool of blue light each night before you go to sleep, and eventually your dreams should be free of malevolence. However, should no change occur in your dream, you should move to the second step.

 ## Psychic self-defence: Method two

Each night, before you recreate your sacred pool, spend a few moments lying peacefully in a relaxed position, breathing slowly and gently, until the mind is totally serene and quiet. In your mind imagine yourself being looked upon by a tall, strong, friendly figure whose form towers over you in a protective stance. This figure can take any form you like, as long as it is strong and powerful, and possesses an overwhelming feeling of friendship and belonging to you. You may not wish to create a human form: a powerful animal such as a bear or a lion or something similar will suffice, as long as you feel comfortable with it and know it to be your friend and protector.

Once you have created this protective thought form, begin to recreate your sacred pool of blue light in front of it. While you picture yourself lying on the golden cross in the sacred pool, see yourself being looked upon by your friend and protector.

Spend as long as it takes to familiarize yourself with the exercise, then allow yourself to drift gently into the realms of slumber, to dream peaceful dreams without threat of any danger.

I would also add that you must know everything about your silent protector. Memorize the features, the shape of the face, the eyes and the nose. Know every characteristic, every feeling, and even endeavour to create a personal fragrance peculiar to your protector. Animate it and endow it with intelligence. Talk to it and imagine it responding telepathically. Over the nights that follow, programme your protector by telling it to guide and protect you while you sleep. Build your relationship slowly, until you feel a deep affinity with it.

The only cautionary note I would add is to create your silent protector in your mind *only* while you are in your bedroom preparing to sleep. This is a vital part of the programming. In this way your silent protector knows that it is to follow you in sleep only, and in those realms it must remain by your side relentlessly.

It is quite difficult for some people to understand just how effective such an exercise in mind power can actually be. The 'things' encountered during sleep are often menacingly created out of potent materials and substances of the lower astral planes. It is from these very materials and substances, therefore, that the weapons to protect oneself must ultimately be created.

It is also a good idea to repeat mentally a prayerful affirmation, such as the Lord's Prayer, or one you have composed yourself. In any case, do not underestimate the power and potency of prayer.

When one has been continuously subjected to psychic attack the aura becomes sluggish and fragmented, particularly around the head.

Some psychic invasions are so subtle that the victim is sometimes unaware of what exactly is happening, and may in fact put the manifestations of such an attack down to illness or simply being run down. Headaches, depression and lethargy may all be the result of psychic invasion and if ignored may, in time, cause serious mental illness. Should you harbour the slightest suspicion that you may be on the receiving end of some kind of psychic attack, do something about it right away. Formulate a working programme of constructive visualization as soon as possible and, if necessary, consult someone who possesses knowledge of the subject.

It is also a good idea to abstain from drinking alcohol, at least until you feel that you have the situation under control. Alcohol and drugs weaken the subtle anatomy, making the aura more susceptible to psychic attack. Those with addictive personalities are prime targets for psychic invasion, as their dependency, no matter how slight, shows mental and personality weakness, which provides easy prey for those seeking either to destroy or to control via psychic means.

Mentally, one should always be on one's guard when working psychically, and also be aware of every area and aspect of one's life. It is not always the intention of the psychic attacker to invade a person's physical body or, for that matter, their mind. There are some who have the power to effect negative changes in another's life by bringing chaos to it. A psychic attack can certainly be directed at a person's situations and circumstances, and can even interfere with, or destroy, relationships and the equilibrium of one's life. I am speaking from experience here, as I personally know only too well just what powerful forces can be in operation when one is subjected to a psychic attack.

From time to time it is a good idea to cleanse the aura with a simple yet effective mental exercise such as the following:

Psychic self-defence: Method three

Sit in a relaxed position in a comfortable chair. Breathe slowly and deeply for a few moments, until the mind is quiet.

In your mind create a curtain of blue light, beginning from

the floor by your feet, all the way up to the ceiling above your head. Light up this curtain of blue with sparkling rays of silver which are bright and shiny, rather like currents of electricity flowing along a bare connection. Allow this curtain of blue light to overwhelm you. Draw it in through your nostrils and down inside yourself, until you are filled with blue.

Very slowly, change the curtain of blue light to red. Allow the red curtain to envelope you as completely as possible. Feel the warmth of the red vibrations against your skin, and see these vibrations as burning away all the negative energy in your aura. Feel the energy pulsating inside you. See yourself being completely revitalized.

Hold this image for a few moments, then gradually change the red curtain of energy to a golden curtain. Allow this to enfold you, at the same time drawing it into your very being. Become totally absorbed by the golden light. Hold it for a few moments, then very slowly allow the whole exercise to fade.

Relax in your chair for a few minutes.

The effects of this exercise may not be felt immediately, but as time passes you will begin to feel mentally stimulated. It also has a remarkable effect upon the practitioner's aura, making the colours therein appear more vibrant and clear. Of course, the effects of this sort of treatment only become more permanent when it is practised regularly, over a period of time. In itself this exercise should not be looked upon as a method of psychic self-defence, but more as an exercise to cleanse the psychic garbage from the aura.

In this respect it is also helpful to drink a few glasses of psychically charged water. As I have said elsewhere in this book, water should be charged simply by passing it from one glass to another, over and over, until the water appears almost to sparkle with vitality. The water will take on the appearance of almost being 'alive' with vitality, and it will taste like fresh mountain spring water.

Other, more specific methods of psychic self-defence appear on the surface to be very general, but in fact they take a great deal of patience and concentration. The art of visualization does not come easily to everyone, but unfortunately it is a prerequisite in one's endeavours to create protective barriers.

The following method is one that can be used in most cases of psychic attack, and it will also strengthen the practitioner's powers of resistance. The exercise itself is quite easy to follow, but it calls for a great deal of dedication. It must be explored fully to enable the practitioner to comprehend the depth of its true meaning. Once the technique has been mastered you will find yourself standing on the threshold of a profound spiritual experience.

Psychic self-defence: Method four

Find a quiet corner and sit in a comfortable chair. It may be a good idea to burn some pleasant incense, any fragrance which is pleasing to your senses.

With your eyes closed begin to breathe slowly and deeply, allowing your stomach to rise as you breathe in, and letting it fall as you breathe out. Breathe in this way for five or ten minutes, then relax with your eyes closed.

Be aware of the space surrounding you, and feel a part of that space. Feel that you are merely occupying your body temporarily, and that you may, therefore, leave it at any time you desire, but you must always return to it, at least for the moment.

See the space surrounding you as sacred and holy ground, and an area in which no one, whether seen or unseen, can move. Allow the space surrounding you to become slowly flooded with vibrant light, coloured with pink. Feel overwhelmed with pink energy, and allow it to infuse your mind, your heart and your soul with gentleness, compassion and love. Make your surrounding space strong and impenetrable, by creating a high wall of golden light around its circumference. Infuse the wall with more energy, making it even more vibrant and powerful. Feel yourself totally submerged in the surrounding pink light, and know without any shadow of a doubt that this is is *your* space, your sacred and holy space, in which nothing and no one can move.

I cannot emphasize enough just how important the imagery is in this sort of exercise. Should the mind wander even for a moment it will cease to be as effective. It must also be practised regularly to enable one's confidence in its effectiveness to develop. Should you only half believe in the protective powers of any of the exercises, their effectiveness will be lessened. Know that they work, and believe in their power.

For general psychic protection many people simply use the 'auric egg'. This can be quite effective.

 # Psychic self-defence: Method five

First of all, decide which colour you feel is powerful enough to afford you spiritual protection. It should of course be one with which you also feel comfortable. Then create an *auric egg* of colour around yourself.

See yourself objectively at first, sitting completely surrounded by the colour of your choice. Then, very slowly, allow the colour to obliterate you completely, until you can only see the coloured egg before you. At this point feel yourself inside the egg, surrounded by the beautiful colour. Make it a strong egg, with plenty of movement in the colour. Allow the energy to infuse you with vitality, to the extent that you can feel yourself almost vibrate.

Continue this visualization for ten minutes. Thereafter it should be practised every day.

Anyone working in the psychic field should always look upon themselves as being carriers of light. Always be mindful that there are those, both in this world and the next, whose sole intention it is to prevent that light from moving into this world. See yourself as a soldier constantly walking beyond enemy lines, remaining ever vigilant. This might sound ridiculous to some, who will feel inclined to pour scorn on what I have said. But believe me, experience alone will make the truth of what I have said clear to you.

Psychic self-defence: Method six

Should you not be fortunate enough to own a meditative pyramid, one that is large enough to sit in, then creating one in the imagination will suffice as a form of protection.

See yourself standing outside a pyramid – a golden pyramid silhouetted against a clear blue sky. See the pyramid shimmering with energy, its walls translucent, rather like mother-of-pearl. In your mind watch the energy pouring through the apex of the pyramid, and see it coming alive.

There is no entrance to the pyramid, so you must simply allow yourself to pass through one of its shimmering walls. You may do so because it is constructed from energy alone. Sit in your pyramid for a few moments imbibing the power and vitality. On the wall of the pyramid facing you there is a large eye staring at you. Make the eye friendly and reassuring.

Clasp your hands in your lap and repeat mentally, 'Oh magic and all-seeing eye, protect me. In my endeavours, watch over me in my sleep.' Again, I must stress the importance of the imagery. Do not allow your attention to wander, even for a single moment.

Remain sitting in your pyramid for ten minutes. Feel totally calm and strong. Then step out through the wall by which you entered, and slowly dissolve the pyramid from your mind.

Although most of these exercises are quite simple, their effectiveness is created from the actual discipline of practice, and the total belief in what the object of the exercise is. The mind is most certainly the common denominator, and you are only as strong as your weakest thought. Through the creative energies of the mind the most powerful weapons are forged.

Certain crystals, too, can be used in a ritualistic approach to psychic protection. For this particular method you will need four clear quartz pointers, and two fairly good-quality pieces of amethyst.

Psychic self-defence:
Method seven

Before you begin the crystals must be programmed or, shall we say, told exactly what to do. First of all, wash them in a mixture of salt and water, with a little cider vinegar added. Rinse them for a few moments under clear tap water then leave them to dry naturally in the sunlight. This process cleanses the crystals of other people's touch, personal fragrances and energies. To programme them, simply place them in your cupped hands on your lap, and sit comfortably in a quiet corner. Meditate upon your crystals, expressing your wishes and infusing them with your will and motives. Spend 10 or 15 minutes on this, then wrap your crystals in a clean white linen cloth and place them somewhere safe, not to be touched by anyone but yourself.

The white cloth is important. Black absorbs emotion and the negative energies of others, while white reflects these, and is of course pure. Try also to keep your crystals away from bright sunlight and other people. Treat them in an almost reverential way, as though they were human and possessed sacred qualities. Approaching your crystals in this way endows them with even more energy and supernatural power. Speak to them in the quietness, tell them your fears and requirements. Ask them for protection at all times. Welcome their friendship and their guidance, and even ask them to unfold their knowledge to you. Meditate upon them as often as possible, as this encourages their inherent qualities to be discharged. The amethyst is often referred to as 'the spiritual stone', and simply holding a piece in the hands produces a calming effect upon the mind. Its inherent properties help to encourage serenity and peace of mind, and also the precipitation of any latent psychic abilities. Being the spiritual stone, it is also an ideal source of protection. Once programmed, the amethyst is capable of releasing amazing energies. Its subtle spiritual properties often encourage the gentle stone to draw to itself the possessor's problems, burdens and dangers. In fact, when a person is overburdened with problems the amethyst has been known to crack or even shatter as a direct result of drawing to itself the negative energies experienced by the owner.

The clear quartz crystal is an extremely powerful stone. Resilient and dynamic, it is often known as the 'enhancing' stone, simply because it increases the energy in anything close to it. because of its inherent spiritual properties, the clear quartz has always been used as a focal point for concentration, and has been used since time immemorial as the powerful crystal from which the crystal ball is made, the means by which many ancient Romany seers have gleaned information from the future. The clear quartz crystal also emanates a powerful protective energy and, combined with the amethyst, is able to create a powerful barrier against evil or negative forces.

For this method, place your clear quartz crystals one in each corner of the room, the points directed towards the centre, where your chair should be.

Sit quietly in your chair, relaxed but with your back straight, shoulders slightly back, and your hands resting, palms up, in your lap with the amethyst piece held lightly between the tips of your fingers.

With your eyes closed, simply breathe in slowly and deeply, all the time being mindful of the amethyst piece in your hands.

Focus your attention first of all on the amethyst stone, calling upon it to release its powers, its inherent properties. Be mindful of the clear quartz pointers in the corners of the room, and feel the energy emanating from them to you and penetrating your very being. Feel the clear quartz crystals creating a circuit of energy across and around the room. Be totally aware of this energy, which appears to pass through your body rather like electricity.

Feel completely secure within the field of energy produced by all the crystals. This energy field appears to be drawn to the amethyst resting in your hands. Feel your whole body glowing, almost alive with energy and power, and for a few moments experience a feeling of bliss, of 'at one-ment' with the universal spirit or universal mind, and know without a doubt that nothing can inflict harm upon you.

When you feel quite comfortable with this exercise and you can see and feel the energy moving freely around the room, create, in your mind, a dome of purple light above your head.

See this dome as pulsating purple light and colour, and allow sunlight to shine through it and cascade down upon the amethyst piece in your hands. See the room aglow with colour and light, and as the sunshine cascades down through the dome upon the amethyst, visualize it breaking up into innumerable colours, which in turn change into a beautiful kaleidoscope of colours which fall about you like minute rainbows. Let the room be alive with colour, light and energy, and in the midst of it all feel a sense of peace overwhelm you.

Sit for a few minutes longer, allowing this emotion to wash over you.

This exercise is very effective for cleansing the aura and for stimulating the creative energies of the mind. It is also an effective method for the creation of a protective barrier when one is subject to a psychic subliminal invasion.

Practise the exercise before going to sleep, then place the clear quartz pointers one at each corner of your bed, points towards each corner. Sleep with the amethyst under your pillow (but only for three nights), then when you awake, sit at the end of your bed with your eyes closed, holding the amethyst in your hands. Breathe in and out for a few moments, slowly and deeply, focusing your complete attention on the amethyst stone, taking from it that which you require to sustain you throughout the day.

Try to begin each day with half a pint of fresh water. Energize it by pouring it from one vessel to another, over and over, backward and forward until the water sparkles with vitality and energy. Drink it slowly to absorb the *Prana*, then relax for a few moments before beginning the day.

chapter 9

OUT OF BODY EXPERIENCES (ASTRAL PROJECTION)

E HEAR A great deal these days about out of body experiences (OBEs). Claims are made by some that they have found themselves floating outside their physical body which they could see below them, either fast asleep in bed, or even lying on an operating table, surrounded by a medical team, undergoing surgery.

Many such experiences have been documented over the last twenty years or so, involving people from many different walks of life, many nationalities, and diverse religious beliefs. Some of the accounts recorded have been given by people who allegedly have had no prior knowledge of such a phenomenon and can involve the elderly, and even very young children.

Even though much of the information contained within the accounts of out of body experiences differs in various ways, all the accounts have a common thread running through them which binds them together in some way, thereby adding credence to the claims made.

Although most of the experiences occur mainly when the body is anaesthetized, there have been accounts of this unusual phenomenon taking place quite spontaneously while the person was fully awake. When the phenomenon is experienced as spontaneously as this, the person to whom it happens can be left in very little doubt that it has occurred while they were fully awake. However, over-activity of the imagination can only be eliminated when the out of body experience has been put to the test. It must be said, however, that six out of ten cases fail this test miserably, even though it is quite straightforward. The person is simply asked to relate that which they observed during the out of body experience, which would not otherwise have been seen had their consciousness remained in the physical body. Furthermore, the person experiencing such a phenomenon also experiences a heightened state of awareness of everything around them, so their consciousness is able to somehow transcend the limitations of the physical body to perceive a fuller geographical landscape, for example, allowing them to experience things taking place in an adjacent road or room. One other thing is common to all those who have experienced any sort of out of body phenomenon, and that is that they find the experience extremely pleasant, and something which they would very much like to replicate.

Before we talk about techniques whereby one can produce such a phenomenon, we must first of all look at the reasons why it happens at all, and also explore the whole concept of the out of body phenomenon and its possibilities.

Even though the out of body experience may be considered a very natural phenomenon, it cannot in any way be thought of as 'normal', and it is certainly not the sort of event one experiences every day of the week. Although it is a phenomenon which can be indicative of certain psychological and emotional illnesses, it is not, strictly speaking, symptomatic of anything in particular. It is certainly a phenomenon that is being widely studied today, and one over which modern day psychologists seem to be more or less split in their opinions, although nearly all are in agreement that such a phenomenon *does* indeed take place.

Before we explore the out of body experience, we must first of all work on the premise that man not only possesses an astral body in the first place, but that he himself is an extremely complex being, possessing other more subtle bodies through which his consciousness can also move and have an experience. In theory, man at any time can experience awareness of any of these bodies, and sometimes does, without actually realizing it. For example, consider a soldier in the grip of attack behind enemy lines. His consciousness is completely focused upon the approaching enemy and the battle at hand, and he does not notice that he has been wounded. Once the battle is over and the enemy has withdrawn, his consciousness once again moves to his physical body and, realizing that he has been injured, he falls into unconsciousness.

During the time the soldier's consciousness was preoccupied he experienced awareness in one of his astral counterparts, thus making the physical body completely anaesthetized to all sensation, and oblivious to anything but the approaching danger.

Although an extremely simple analogy, it is, I feel, one which illustrates the concept of shifting consciousness perfectly well.

Another example is that experienced in deep sleep when one is dreaming. Here again the sleeper is completely oblivious to both his body and his surroundings, and experiences awareness in a state of consciousness over which he appears to have little or no control. If the sleeper were able to control his consciousness during the time he was asleep, there would be limitless possibilities and greater freedom of awareness available to him. By developing control of the consciousness, particularly during the sleep state, man would be able to access states of awareness in which time and space as we conceive it to be would simply not exist. I am, of course, speaking of the 'subjective' levels of the astral world, in which the geography is peculiar to that part of the astral universe alone and in no way bears any relation to the geography of the physical world.

Because of the very nature of the astral plane, until one develops the ability of the consciousness to function with a more controlled freedom in it, one's sensory awareness of the astral plane can only be described as nebulous. However, once such development takes place, it is as though a grey veil rises to reveal before the consciousness a new and vibrant landscape of colour, form and sound.

Various techniques can be employed in order to project the astral body, but before any of these are explored one should learn to focus the consciousness upon the self in a simple meditative exercise.

 Technique one

Step One

Sit in a relaxed posture, preferably on a straight-backed chair, with your back straight and hands resting lightly in the lap.

Breathe slowly and deeply, making quite sure that the inhalations and exhalations are evenly spaced. Make the mind as quiet as possible. Remain in this position for a few minutes, until you are totally relaxed. Then rise from your chair and walk into an adjacent room.

Take note of everything you can see there, making a clear picture in your mind so that you know where everything is, and can recall it in your imagination later. Return to your chair in your quiet room and relax once again. Begin to breathe slowly and deeply, summoning all the power you can into your solar plexus. Discharge this power on the exhalations, while creating in your mind a clear image of yourself standing in front of you and facing away, so that you have a clear view of your own back.

Try to see yourself clearly, dressed in the same clothes that you are wearing now, and watch yourself walking away, towards the door. When you can see yourself reaching the door, freeze the image of yourself, breathe in deeply, and on the exhalation allow the image of yourself to fade.

Step Two

Rise from your chair and wander once again into the adjacent room. Repeat the motions of looking round and checking the position of everything in the room. Use all your senses to accurately record the full picture. Familiarize yourself with any fragrances, pay attention to colours, and make a special note of the exact position of furniture. In other words, refresh your mental picture of exactly how everything looks. Return to your chair in your quiet room and relax again, with your eyes closed.

Breathe slowly and deeply once more, paying attention to the streams of vitality flowing in through your nostrils and down into your solar plexus. Try to become accustomed to breathing in this way, summoning all the power you can into your solar plexus. Remember, as you breathe in let your stomach rise, and when you breathe out let it fall. Each time you exhale, discharge the power, simultaneously recreating the image of yourself standing in the doorway ready to leave. See yourself passing through the door and out of sight.

Still totally relaxed, imagine yourself now as the image you have created of yourself. Allow yourself mentally to move into the adjacent room. Once there, stand for a few moments and look around. Feel as though you are actually there: smell the fragrances, see the colours of everything around you, note the position of the furniture. Move about in the room, allowing your eyes to scan your surroundings, before slowly moving back towards the door. Stand in the doorway for a few moments and take a last look around before leaving the room and returning to your chair. Before opening your eyes sit quietly for a few moments, breathing gently and rhythmically. When you feel ready to conclude the exercise breathe in deeply one last time, and with the exhalation discharge the whole picture from your mind, and open your eyes.

Once you have finished it is vitally important not to go over the exercise in your mind. Instead, direct your mind completely away from it, and make yourself a cup of tea.

Even if your powers of imagination are extremely good, little will be accomplished from one or two sittings. To achieve full astral projection the experiment must be conducted over and over until very little concentration is needed on your part, and the imagery pulls you along automatically, of its own accord, and not the other way around. When this happens you will know it. The imagery you create in your mind will suddenly become intensified and you will experience a pleasant feeling of floating. This is the all-important point at which the astral body seeks separation. When this sensation is experienced many people become excited, inhibiting the process so that it simply does not progress any further. Once you experience this sensation of buoyancy try to remain completely calm and relaxed. Should this prove difficult – the excitement and anticipation is often extremely difficult to contain – it is quite acceptable to suspend the exercise until later, when you have had some time to look objectively at what has happened.

Remember: full projection does take time and a lot of practice. However, once it has been confidently achieved, the boundaries can be extended. Arrangements can be made to travel astrally to the home of a friend with whom you feel comfortable and who you can trust, someone who lives only a short distance away. Remember: the experiment must still be carried out in the same way, and the exact same procedure must be followed.

Step Three

Take a casual stroll from your house to your friend's, making a mental note of everything you can see on your journey: The other houses and the way in which they are painted, the gardens and traffic, children playing in the street, people passing by. In other words mentally record everything so that you can recall it clearly in your imagination later on. Make the journey several times before beginning the exercise.

Arrange the co-operation of a friend. Walk to your friend's house and ring the doorbell. Pass through their door, move into their house and into the room they will be sitting in. When you feel ready, and the exercise has been set up in your mind, follow it in your imagination in exactly the same way as you did with the first experiment, going slowly through it stage by stage, until you feel confident that the imagery you have made of yourself is now strong enough to commence the journey to your friend's home.

Should your attention wander at some point while visualizing yourself making the short journey to your friend's house, imagine yourself walking back to your own home, passing through your front door and returning to your chair. Suspend the exercise until later.

You may initially like to consider not completing the exercise in one sitting. Go through it in stages. Let the first stage be moving to your front door; the second stage as far as the garden gate; the third stage walking a few yards from your house. At the fourth stage, see yourself walking half-way down the street. At the fifth stage, see yourself reaching your friend's front door. At the final stage, enter your friend's home, and see yourself walking into the room where they are sitting.

It may all sound fairly straightforward and simple, but believe me it is not. This technique calls for a great deal of practice and patience, with total dedication. It may, of course, take you a comparatively short time to achieve full astral projection. It all depends on your ability to project your imagination, and on the latent potential which you already possess. You may even find yourself projecting spontaneously, without going through the whole procedure of visualization. On the other hand, it may well take you a long time to achieve. Whichever category you fall into, try not to lose interest, and practise as often as possible, as this is the only way in which results can be positively and successfully achieved.

It may well be that you would simply like to develop or even improve your ability to travel astrally when you sleep. In this case a slightly different approach is needed.

 Technique two

Step One

First of all, make a note of all your dreams for a full month by keeping a note pad and pen by your bed. Whatever time you retire to bed, set your alarm clock to wake you approximately two and a half hours later, at which time you should make a note of anything you can remember dreaming, no matter how vague. Upon waking in the morning, immediately write down what you experienced when you were asleep.

Set your alarm in this way every night for a period of one month, or until you have acquired the habit of waking at this time.

Step Two

In bed each night, before going to sleep, lie comfortably on your back, preferably with no pillows beneath your head. Focus your attention at a chosen spot on the ceiling and stare intently at this spot without blinking or moving your gaze even for a brief moment. Still gazing at the spot on the ceiling, become conscious of your breathing. As you breathe in feel your abdominal area filling with power and vitality, and on the exhalation feel yourself sinking completely into the bed. Allow this slow and rhythmical breathing to continue for several minutes until you are fully relaxed. Continue to resist the temptation to close your eyes or even to move your gaze. As you breathe in deeply, feel as though your whole body is being filled with a vitality which gradually makes your body feel light, and as you exhale feel serene and calm. With each inhalation feel your body become almost weightless, and every time you exhale allow yourself to feel more and more at peace. When a state of serenity has been achieved, slowly close your eyes and lie still and calm for a few moments.

Focus all your energies on the solar plexus. Visualize these energies streaming from that area to form a clearly defined, replicated image of yourself, hovering horizontally a few feet above you. When you can see this picture clearly in your mind's eye, hold it for a few minutes, then slowly bring it down towards you again, feeling it being drawn once more, as energy, into your solar plexus.

Practise this exercise each night before going to sleep, but still continue to note down all your dreams. Keep a careful record also of anything else you experience when you are asleep.

Step Three

After a few weeks, when you feel completely confident in your mental imagery of yourself floating above the bed, you should mentally begin to programme the image of yourself in the following way. Concentrate all your energies on the replicated image of yourself, telling it forcefully exactly what you require of it, and what it is that you are trying to achieve. For example, '*I wish to have total control of my dreams, and to remember everything about them.*'

Repeat this phrase over and over again, while mentally holding the image of yourself floating above you while you are lying on the bed. Use it as an affirmation with which to programme the image you have created of yourself. By repeating your wishes over and over again, the mental command is gradually taken up by the subconscious mind, and is then passed on to the mental aspects of the astral body.

Practised repeatedly over a period of time, you will be amazed at the results of this exercise. Note how your dream patterns change. Once the desired results have been successfully achieved you may wish to programme not only the way you dream, but the kind of dreams you have, and also to improve your memory of them. Simply tell the created image of yourself what to do, such as, 'In my dreams I wish to go to America to visit my cousin, and I wish to have total recall of all that takes place.'

I cannot emphasize enough the importance of the mental repetition of the affirmation, as this infuses the entire exercise with energy and power, and almost lends your astral image wings.

You may of course like to experiment with this technique by making prior arrangements to meet with a friend on the astral plane.

Technique three

Step One

Tell your friend to spend some time thinking about you just before they go to sleep. Arrange to meet them in the sleep state at a particular destination such as beneath the town hall clock at, for instance, 3a.m.

Having gone through the same procedure of creating the image of yourself floating above you while you are on the bed, allow your mind to see the mental image of the town hall clock, making the time on it the time that it really is at that moment. Make the imagery very bright and clear in your mind, and focus your attention on it until five minutes have elapsed on the clock. Your friend should try to imagine you standing under the town hall clock. They should try to hold this picture in their mind for five minutes before going to sleep.

Step Two

Let your thoughts move away from the picture of the town hall and focus on your breathing. Breathe in slowly and deeply, allowing your stomach to rise, and breathe out watching it fall. Continue this breathing for five minutes, then gradually allow your mind to drift from your breathing, very slowly creating the clear image of yourself floating above you as you lie on the bed. Make this image very clear in your mind.

Once you feel that the picture is strong enough, and you are confident that it is going to work, set about the programming: 'I want to travel to the town hall clock at three o'clock to meet my friend. I want to experience this as strongly and as vividly as though I were there physically, and I wish to recall everything that takes place.' Repeat this mental affirmation several times before allowing yourself to fall asleep.

You should keep a careful record of everything that takes place. It may take a few months, or even longer, before anything positive happens. On the other hand results may be produced in a very short time. It is doubtful, however, that anything other than a pleasant or unusual dream will be experienced on the first night, but practice and determination will eventually produce the desired, successful results.

You should, of course, compare notes with your friend to see if you have been successful in your astral rendezvous. Tell them everything you experienced, and what you noticed – where they were standing, what they were wearing, etc.

Remember: it is a good idea to seek protection before entering into sleep by offering a short, meaningful prayer – a form of request for protection from those whom you believe to be guiding and watching over you in your endeavours.

I should point out that usually the first thing to be developed with such a technique is the ability to programme and remember your dreams. Consequently your dreams will become much more lucid, this being an indication that the astral body is beginning to detach itself more and more under your conscious control.

Here I must sound a cautionary note: should you begin to experience disturbing nightmares it would be wise to leave the technique alone for a few weeks. This could be an indication that negative energies have somehow found their way into your auric field, in which case your mental energies need to be directed into other things, at least until everything has settled down again. The energy levels do normally recover by themselves, unless of course you are feeling a little run-down physically, or perhaps being subjected to some degree of psychological and emotional stress.

If you do have any history of mental illness you would be wise to leave this particular area alone, as it could be detrimental to your psychological health.

chapter 10

PSYCHIC HEALING

NO BOOK ON psychic development would be complete without some mention of healing, and although many books have been written on this extensive subject, with its many forms and techniques, I would like to explore with you some methods of psychic healing, and perhaps offer you some guidelines for the development of such an ability.

A psychic healing practitioner is someone who possesses the ability to draw upon large and powerful reservoirs of energy from outside him or herself, and to transmute and discharge that energy for the purpose of restoring the health and vitality of another person's physical body.

This method of healing is not to be confused with that which is termed 'spiritual healing', which employs the guidance, wisdom and knowledge of a discarnate agency. While the person receiving spiritual healing does not have to possess any particular religious views, and does not even have to believe in the effectiveness of spiritual healing (spiritual healing works on animals and children and is, therefore, not dependent upon faith or belief in God), the practitioner of spiritual healing does have to have some form of deep spiritual belief in an omnipotent, omnipresent power.

The psychic healer's abilities, however, are not dependent upon such a belief, although he or she does need to believe that they have the ability to transmute an incoming cosmic force, and are able to channel such a force for the purpose of healing.

In a previous chapter, I have already defined the nature of *Prana*, and explained that this is the word used in the philosophy of yoga to designate all energy in the universe. *Prana* is not only the integrating principle of all things both animate and inanimate, and therefore to be found working through all forms of matter, but it is also the perpetuator and sustainer of all life, and when *Prana* ceases to be present death ultimately occurs. Consequently, when the levels of *Prana* are lowered in the physical body for some reason or another, the resultant manifestations become apparent in diseases of either the body or the mind.

Eastern yogic masters know that by increasing and controlling the in-coming streams of *Prana*, they can not only promote longevity, but they can also retain their youthful appearance, health and vitality. Although the fundamental principles underlying the retention of *Prana* involve specific breathing techniques from a system termed 'Pranayama' (the control of *Prana*), it is understood by Yogic masters that there are some people who quite naturally bring in and retain large streams of this force, and just by being in the presence of these people we experience an overwhelming sense of invigoration, particularly when we are feeling run-down or simply unwell.

The fact that some people appear to possess this potent force in large amounts has nothing to do with their anatomical or physical appearance or make-up. I have often seen small, slightly built people who have the psychic appearance of being almost like 'electricity'. A great many athletes possess strong currents of *Prana* in their bodies, particularly those who work in water, this being quite a powerful source of *Prana*, and a potent agency through which *Prana* works.

Those who work with soil, too, such as farmers or dedicated gardeners, nearly always possess strong currents of *Prana*, which very often gives them a serene, calm appearance.

As I have said previously, *Prana* is stored in the solar plexus from where it is continually distributed throughout the body, and drawn automatically to the organs where it is needed. Normally any depletion of *Prana* in the body is restored through the natural process of atmospheric recharging, but in the case of serious illness the depletion of the body's reserves continues until death eventually occurs.

You should now have a reasonable knowledge of *Prana* and how it can enhance the quality of our lives, so let us now consider the various methods of healing with it.

Technique one

This is a simple experiment to enable you to experience the manifestation of *Prana* in your hands.

Sit comfortably on a straight-backed chair and place your hands gently on your solar plexus. Close your eyes. Feel the pulse of energy in the abdominal area and, as you allow your hands to remain in this position, so you may notice their temperature gradually changing. If, after five minutes, nothing has happened, shake your hands vigorously for a few minutes, allowing all your fingers to snap together in the process. Now place your hands gently on your forehead, and feel your fingers tingling with vitality, almost coming alive with energy. As you hold them against your forehead notice how the tingling appears to affect your head, as your fingers send streams of *Prana* into it. Once the tingling has ceased, shake your hands vigorously once again for a few moments. You should then place your fingertips gently on your solar plexus. Notice the sensation in your hands. They should feel 'alive' with energy

This exercise creates a sudden rush of *Prana* from the head to the solar plexus. The *Prana* can then be conveyed to another person to ease any pain they may be experiencing.

Practise this method before applying your hands to someone who is feeling run-down, anxious, or perhaps in constant pain in some part of the body.

It is not necessary to apply your hands to a specific part of a person's body, as *Prana* creates a powerful circuit in the whole organism, and immediately finds its own level in the body.

Pranic healing is not, generally speaking, a curative method, but it is certainly known to create such movements of energy in the body as to move blockages, thereby normalizing the body's natural self-healing processes. It certainly has quite a powerful effect on pain, and when applied will ease most pain almost immediately.

The magnetic force of *Prana* is, as I have said elsewhere in this book, the fundamental principle underlying most hypnotic treatments. Franz Mesmer, the innovator of what was termed 'mesmerism', which was one of the earlier forms of what we know today as hypnotism, and which was named after him, made an extensive study of this concept.

To truly effect a hypnotic trance-like state, the practitioner must understand the concept of in-flowing energy, and must learn to project that energy with each intonation of the phrases used to promote the trance-like state. Mesmer knew that unless the practitioner of mesmerism was able to project his personal magnetic forces, the only thing which would transpire between the patient and the practitioner would be a collection of words and phrases.

There is a very definite psychology, too, underlying psychic healing which can be extremely powerful when applied in the correct way. A mother will often rub the winter chill from a child's cold hands saying, 'There you are, now your hands are lovely and warm.'

The rubbing motion of the mother's hands not only improves the child's circulation, but through them she also imparts a stream of *Prana*, which she psychologically enforces with a reassuring statement.

Prana also responds greatly to the imagination, and can be coloured with a specific mission in mind.

 ## Technique two

Seat your patient on a straight-backed chair and stand behind them. Close your eyes for a few moments and place your hands gently on your patient's shoulders, allowing your thoughts to blend completely with theirs. Once you have attuned yourself to the patient's body shake your hands vigorously by your side for a minute or so, and then point both index fingers to the ground, either side of you, imagining streams of energy being drawn up through the extended fingers.

Still holding the fingers rigid, slowly raise your hands and place one either side of the patient's head, with your index fingers pointing just behind the ears. Breathe in slowly, and as you exhale mentally discharge the energy from your fingers into the patient's head.

Repeat this process five or six times, always beginning with the vigorous shaking of your hands, thereby stimulating the flow of *Prana*.

If a patient is suffering from some form of infection and has a high temperature, follow the same procedure, but this time visualize the energy which is drawn in through your fingers as being coloured with a vibrant blue. When you discharge the energy into the patient's head, again see that it has a powerful blue force as it streams through your fingertips, filling the patient's head completely with the colour of vibrant blue. Should the patient's temperature be low for some reason, use the same method again, and simply colour the force red.

Conclude the treatment by sweeping your hands up and down the patient's body, either side of them, without touching them, from the head to the hips. Then move to the side of the patient and repeat the sweeping process down their front and back.

These cleansing passes of the hands have a stimulating effect on a person's aura, and also encourage the healing force to circulate more freely throughout the subtle anatomy.

When a person is recovering from illness and is therefore very low in vitality, the healing processes can be encouraged by the use of a very simple treatment which I call 'auric and chakra massage'.

This not only has a deep stimulating effect upon the person's energy field, but it also helps to create movement in the channels along which energy is conveyed around the body.

By introducing a little colour into the treatment the person's energy levels are suddenly increased, and the whole person (body, mind and spirit) experiences a sudden rush of energy, as though they have been bathed in a powerful beam of cosmic light.

The healers ability to visualize is extremely beneficial in the transmission of the healing forces and will aid the precipitation of *Prana*.

Technique three

For this method the patient should lie either on the floor or, ideally, on a therapy bed.

Reassure them as much as possible by talking them through relaxation until they feel completely serene and calm. Stand or kneel beside the patient, whichever is appropriate. Place one hand on their forehead, and the other on their solar plexus. Remain in this position until you can feel warmth in your hands. Then withdraw your hands.

Now, place your left hand over the patient's forehead, without touching it, at a distance of approx. 1in. (2.5cm) from it. Place your right hand over your left hand, again approximately one inch away, without touching it.

Begin the healing treatment by very slowly moving your left hand in a circular, clockwise motion, and moving your right hand over your left hand, in a circular, anti-clockwise motion. Keep the movements of your hands slow and even, with the fingers on both hands spread apart. Concentrate the movements of both hands over the patient's forehead for at least one minute. Next, gradually move your hands down to the throat area. Apply the treatment to this spot for a further minute, before moving your hands down to the heart area.

Remember: the movements of your hands are of paramount importance, in order to create movement in the subtle energies of the body.

Keep the left hand moving slowly with a clockwise motion, and the right hand moving slowly with an anti-clockwise motion. Move your hands down to the area just above the naval, remaining there for one minute. Then move your hands down to the naval area, and spend one minute there. Finally, move to the lowest part of the trunk, again for one minute.

The first part of this treatment (as above) should take eight to ten minutes. The whole treatment should then be repeated, beginning once again with the forehead. However, before you begin again, rest your left hand on the patient's forehead, and

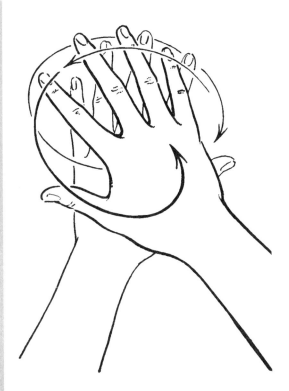

your right hand on their solar plexus. Remain in this position as you intuitively determine which colours should be used in the second part of the treatment.

Close your eyes and be guided to the appropriate colours by your intuition. Simply flick through the colours of the spectrum in your mind, and see which one stands out the strongest. This sounds much more difficult than it really is. Once you have concluded the first part of the treatment you will find that you have become closely attuned to your patient, and will just 'know' which colour to use.

Having intuitively selected the appropriate colour ray, repeat the healing process. Begin by moving the left hand in a clockwise motion as before, and the right hand, placed over the left without touching it, in an anti-clockwise motion. A few seconds into the treatment begin to transmit the chosen colour mentally, by visualizing it being projected from between your eyebrows, passing through your circling hands, and on into the patient.

Remember: it is important that you do not allow your mind to wander from the imagery, as this lapse in concentration only dissipates the force in a negative, needless way. It is also better to use more than one colour in the treatment – but at all times be guided by your intuition. Work your way slowly down the body, then ask the patient to turn over onto their stomach, and repeat the process.

Begin this time with the back of the head, and conclude with the base of the spine. When the treatment is finished sweep your hands up and down the patient's body, shaking them slightly as you do so. These sweeping passes over the body have the effect of sealing the circulating force. They also have a strong cleansing effect upon the patient's aura.

The more you practise the above method, the more you may feel able to do with it. You may even feel that you need to modify it in some way. This really does not matter, as long as the motions of the hands, moving in opposite directions, are retained in the exercise.

This treatment is also beneficial for those with respiratory conditions, stomach or digestive problems, and in the easing of debilitating spinal conditions.

Remember: should you lack confidence in your skills as a psychic healer, this will interfere with your ability to project the psychic force used in the treatment. Equally, if you have no confidence in what you are doing, your patient will lack confidence in it, too. So be certain that you know you do have the power within you to heal. Have faith and confidence, and the power will be more effective.

Administering psychic healing on a regular basis, allowing yourself little or no time to recover your energies, will very quickly send you into poor health. Once your levels of vitality have been allowed to fall below a certain degree, you may have extreme difficulty in raising them again. So you must safeguard against a depletion in your own vitality. Tiredness is one of the primary symptoms of a depletion in the vital force, as are irritability and nervousness. Should you allow this state to persist, you will find yourself becoming more susceptible to illnesses of a more serious nature.

Take time away from your healing practice. Take long walks in the park or countryside, enjoying plenty of fresh air. Eat lots of fruit and fresh green vegetables, and try to drink at least two pints of water charged with *Prana* each day. Charge your water in the way I have already mentioned, pouring it from one vessel to another, passing it backwards and forwards, over and over, through the air, until it has the appearance of being almost alive with vitality. When drinking it, hold the water in your mouth for a few moments, washing it around the tongue to absorb the *Prana*, before eventually swallowing it.

Rest as much as possible, particularly before administering healing treatment. Try to retire to bed as early as possible.

The most effective exercise for replenishing the nervous system with vitality is one I often use.

 ## Exercise 30

Sit in an erect posture with your back straight. Place your fingertips gently on your solar plexus. Breathe in very slowly, imagining streams of *Prana*, like white light, passing through your nostrils and down into your lungs, then into your solar plexus, where it is immediately taken up by your fingertips. When your breath has been completed, hold it for a few moments, and then place your fingertips against your forehead, between your brows. Convey the white light in your fingertips to your forehead. Holding your fingertips against your forehead, breathe the white light out through your fingertips and into your head, flooding it completely with vitality. When all the breath has been expelled, hold it for a few moments, and then return your fingertips to your solar plexus.

Repeat the exercise several times, until you experience a tingling sensation either in your hands, or on your forehead, or even both.

I must stress the importance of the imagery here, as it is this which adds force to the effectiveness of the exercise. You should not allow your mind to wander from the visualization even for a moment, as this would merely defeat the object of the exercise, which is to restore vitality to the nervous system and replenish the depleted levels of energy in the subtle channels of the organism.

Mastering the technique of accumulating great stores of *Prana* in the body is something that develops of its own accord over a period of time; that is, once you have come to know exactly what this energy is, and have begun to use it in your healing practices.

Of course, as I have already explained, the body's in-pouring streams of *Prana* may be encouraged by the use of specific breathing methods and visualization techniques. Once this has been achieved, streams of *Prana* may be directed at a sick person, accompanied by a specific mental command, in order to encourage the body's healing process.

This method calls for a great deal of concentration, and confidence in one's healing abilities, but once it has been administered correctly, positive results are nearly always achieved almost immediately.

 ## Exercise 31

Before administering healing, sit comfortably on a straight-backed chair, with the mind totally focused on yourself and the powers you possess within. Breathe rhythmically for a few minutes, paying particular attention to your inhalations and the in-coming force. Allow your diaphragm to expand as you breathe in slowly and deeply, and feel invigorated as your body absorbs the in-pouring *Prana*.

Extend your arms, at 45 degrees, with the palms of your hands facing inwards, and on a slow inhalation of breath, draw them slowly inwards and place the palms of your hands against your chest. Exhale fully.

Extend your arms once again, the palms of your hands facing inwards, and repeat the process.

Repeat the exercise five or six times, simply following the slow rhythm of your breathing, and then gradually begin to introduce specific revitalizing colours into the in-flowing *Prana*. This time, when you inhale, imagine streams of pink energy flowing into your body. Watch it carefully, passing through your nostrils and down into your lungs. When you exhale, see all the waste and toxins pouring out from you. Give these a murky green or yellow colour.

Continue this exercise for a further five to eight minutes and then relax.

You should feel fully 'charged' after this exercise, and ready to commence the healing treatment.

It is not enough simply to administer healing. There must be some verbal reassurance and interaction with your patient. Should they feel ill at ease with you, the process of healing will be restricted as a consequence of the mental barriers which the patient subconsciously erects as a form of defence.

Nor should you begin the treatment as soon as your patient enters the room. Take time to exchange general conversation and, above all, do not appear too clinical in your approach, as this can be extremely off-putting to many people.

It is important to rest for a time before the healing treatment begins in any case of serious illness, and it is advisable to eat only sparingly before administering healing.

Prepare yourself mentally for the patient, creating 'mind pictures' of the health condition you wish to achieve.

The following treatment may be applied to most health conditions, but it may be particularly effective in the easing of pain, especially where the lungs and stomach areas are involved.

Technique four

Step One

Ask the patient to lie on their stomach. Standing alongside the patient, with your eyes closed, move your hands fairly quickly across and up and down their body, at a distance of approx. 2–3in. (5–8cm) from it, without touching. 'Scan' the patient's body in this way until you feel intuitively guided to a specific part of their anatomy, and then simply hold your hands steadily over that point.

At first, do not think of anything in particular, but simply allow your hands to remain in that position. The patient's body will draw the *Prana* it needs from your hands – you may soon notice them becoming warm.

At this point, focus all your energies into your hands, sending the mental command to the patient's body: 'Pain be released. Pain be released.'

Repeat this mentally, over and over again, until you feel impressed to move on. Continue to scan the body with your hands, allowing your intuition to take you mentally to where the healing is needed.

This may sound fanciful and far-fetched to some people, but believe me, it is an extremely effective method, and one that can create a great deal of energy which is discharged into the patient.

Once you feel that the 'scanning' process has been exhausted, move on to the next step.

Step Two

Still standing alongside the patient, shake your hands vigorously by your sides until they feel 'alive' with energy. While your hands are still tingling place them gently on the back of the patient's head. Hold your hands in that position until the tingling sensation has ceased, and then withdraw them from the patient's head.

Shake your hands vigorously once again for a full minute. This time, place your left hand on the left side of the patient's back, around the lung area, and your right hand on the right side of their back. Hold your hands in that position until the tingling in them has ceased. Next, make sweeping passes up and down the spine, from the base of the skull to the base of the spine, imagining the patient bathed in the colour green. Infuse this colour mentally, with a force that becomes more potent with each exhalation of your breath. Continue this for as long as you feel necessary, then ask the patient to turn on to their back.

Repeat the process, allowing yourself to be intuitively guided.

The same procedure should be followed each time, regardless of whether or not you already know what is wrong with the patient. Where psychic healing is concerned treatment should be applied to the whole person, as opposed to the affected part of the body. However, particular attention *may* be focused on the troubled part of a person's anatomy, just to encourage the healing process.

The head, the lungs, the spine and the stomach areas play an extremely important role in the assimilation and transmutation of energy. By encouraging the movement of the force in these anatomical areas, normalization of the body's natural processes may be effected. Particular attention should always be paid to the stomach area, as this is usually where most of a person's energy reserves are stored, and a depletion in energy levels is usually first experienced in this area. Therefore, by focusing the healing at this point (stomach), and accompanying it with a specific revitalizing colour, such as orange, the energy levels may be restored, and the healing process encouraged.

Transmitting colour mentally means that the shade and intensity can be altered immediately, and combinations of colours can be introduced instantly, without the patient even realizing it.

Experimentation is important when working with colour, and a process of elimination should be applied when treating certain illnesses with colour. You may even find that the way you work in the psychic healing field is unique to *you*; as long as you achieve positive results, it really does not matter.

The following short table may be of some help to you initially. I have listed various colours alongside the conditions which usually respond positively to them.

Colour   Condition

Colour	Condition
Red	Lethargy; blood disorders; lack of appetite; poor circulation.
Blue	Painful conditions affecting any part or organ of the body; psychological problems; promotes general toning and calming of the nerves.
Yellow	Liver; kidneys; bowels; some lung conditions; where energy is needed.
Green	Heart; lungs; low body weight; run down; eye problems; nervous conditions.
Orange	Lack of energy; loss of vitality; pneumonia; some stomach problems.
Violet	A good all-round healing colour. Promotes balance in the body and the mind; calms the nervous system; aids general recovery from illness.

Combinations of colours may be used when mentally transmitting. You would obviously have great difficulty imagining two colours simultaneously, but, by alternating their mental transmission, they can form an extremely powerful force in the treatment of some health conditions.

Red combined with green, for example, is effective in the treatment of jaundice, and bright red combined with orange is very effective in the treatment of exhaustion.

Remember: your powers of visualization are important in this form of psychic healing treatment, as is your ability to focus all your powers into one specific point.

chapter 11

MEDITATION –
THE KEY TO
SELF-MASTERY

HEN I SPEAK of meditation, I am talking about a specific system of mental exercises in which discipline is exerted over one's mental processes with the sole object of cultivating a much greater awareness of the reality of the soul, and its independence of the body, so aiding in the precipitation of consciousness.

As this book is about developing your psychic powers, we will explore all the possibilities of meditation, and how exactly it can work for you as a means through which such powers may be mastered.

Although group meditation can be very effective when one is seeking to attain a higher level of consciousness with the sole intention of developing psychic abilities, I believe that certain methods of meditation are simply not suitable for some people, who may find the practice, for example, in a group, uncomfortable in one way or another. The effects of meditation certainly vary from person to person, and are often dependent upon the individual's personality, metabolism, mental and emotional processes, and their ability to concentrate. For example, some people may find it almost impossible to hold an abstract thought in the mind for a minute, let alone for ten minutes, and may prefer to gaze at a geometric pattern, which takes little or no concentration at all.

The whole psychology of the person must first be studied, whatever technique of meditation is used and, if necessary, the method should be modified to suit them.

Generally speaking, any mental exercise that controls the thought processes can be considered to be meditation. Even reading a book may, in theory, be considered a form of meditation, as this often holds the concentration, making one oblivious to all else around.

You can be quite certain that as long as the correct technique of meditation is used, the benefits will be experienced at all levels of the user's existence, and may even in the long term effect some profound changes in the individual's situation and circumstances, by aiding the cultivation of a whole new and more creative approach to their life.

The 'three-fold meditation' approach is one technique which most people find of great benefit when endeavouring to sharpen the senses. It is a technique which encapsulates the whole person, bringing together the emotional, mental and spiritual aspects of one's nature. It involves three steps: *Contemplation*, *Concentration*, and *Meditation*.

 ## Exercise 32

Begin, as always, with some rhythmic breathing, so as to slow everything down and reduce the level of activity in the mind. Check that your posture is comfortable, and that the back is straight with the shoulders slightly back. Rest your hands lightly in your lap.

Step One: Contemplation

Focus your thoughts on your reason for meditating, asking yourself what it is that you are seeking to achieve. Try not to make your reason too complicated.

Having decided exactly what it is, establish it fully in your mind, and for five minutes or more contemplate its possibilities. In your contemplative state look at yourself objectively and try to see yourself as others see you. Should the picture you have of yourself reveal someone who is weak and lacking in confidence, change this image into someone who is strong, confident, even dynamic. Spend some time on this until you have a clear picture of the new you in your mind.

The period of contemplation is used to prepare the mind for the next phase, that of concentration. Concentrating for any length of time can be very tiring, but a few moments spent in contemplation gently brings the meditator into the correct frame of mind, making their ability to concentrate a little sharper.

Step Two: Concentration

Focus your gaze on a point of space in front of you. For a few moments hold it steady, as always resisting the temptation to blink. When your eyes begin to water, and you can no longer gaze, allow your eyes to slowly close.

At this point you should focus your attention on the top of your head. Allow your attention to penetrate the top of your skull, imagining a small violet, spiralling light, just below the surface of the crown. See it glowing brightly and swirling with a clockwise motion.

Allow your focus to move through the swirling violet light, down to the space just between your brows, and become totally aware of a deep blue pulsating point of light. Allow this to hold your attention for a few moments, then gradually move your focus inwardly to the throat area. Here you become conscious of a bright blue radiation of light, full of movement and appearing almost luminous. Focus on this for a few moments.

Next, allow your attention to pass inwardly to the region of the heart. Allow yourself to be overwhelmed by a beautiful shade of aquamarine. Feel it quickening your senses. Experience this colour at an emotional level, and then slowly move your focus to the area just below the left side of your rib cage, where you become totally conscious of a sparkling, deep yellow, swirling light. Focus your attention on the yellow light, and be aware of it expanding as it moves with a clockwise motion. Focus on it for a few moments longer, mentally drinking in the vibrant stimulation of the yellow.

Move your attention to the naval area and become aware of a feeling of strength and clarity of thought. Allow your attention to be drawn inside this point, and to be over-whelmed by its sheer strength and vitality. Imbibe its power.

Move slowly to the base of your spine, allowing your attention to be gradually drawn into a fiery glow. Feel the spontaneous energy as your consciousness is drawn deeper into this red, fiery whirlpool, from which you should be conscious of streams of vitality moving up your spine to the crown of your head.

Spend a few moments watching all these beautiful colours individually, before seeing them collectively manifest in a huge pool of colour in front of you. See this swirling pool as though you are standing next to it, watching the sunlight playing across the surface of the water. See the reflection of the sun setting in the centre of the pool. Allow your attention to be drawn down through it, until you feel the colours all around you.

Hold this experience for five or ten minutes before allowing it to dissolve completely.

Step Three: Meditation

Find yourself sitting at the bottom of a pool, able to breathe and to see flashes of colour produced by the setting sun above you. Allow your attention to be focused on a white lotus flower in front of you, on the bed of the pool. Pick it up in cupped hands and see yourself holding it upwards, your arms stretched out towards the cascading light.

Allow yourself mentally to rise to your feet, and see yourself float to the surface of the pond, still clutching the beautiful white lotus flower. Allow yourself mentally to emerge into the beautiful light produced by the setting sun, burning like a huge ball of fire on the horizon. Hold the lotus flower up to the fiery sky which is awash with purple, green, red, yellow and orange flames.

> Hold the lotus flower close to your breast, and when you again offer your hands to the sun, the lotus flower has been replaced by a white butterfly which moves off gracefully on the gentle breeze. See its gossamer-like wings, iridescent in the glowing red sunlight, and watch it as it moves away into nothingness.
>
> Sit for a moment before allowing the meditation to fade gently from your mind. Relax.

This particular exercise is an experience in colour. As well as having a profound effect upon the senses, it helps to clear the auric colours, making them sharper and much more intense.

Through meditation, the mind may exert a greater authority over the aura and the subtle anatomy, and its practice will also aid the movement of energy through the various channels of vitality.

Activating and releasing the inherent qualities of the individual chakras may be achieved with the use of various mental techniques, but their activation can be initiated with a method of mental activity specifically designed for such a purpose.

Each chakra is represented symbolically by a geometric pattern called a 'Yantra', which externally symbolizes the inherent qualities of each centre for the purpose of meditation.

These yantras may be used alone, or combined with the sound of the chakra, which is called a 'Bija Mantra'. Yantras and Bija Mantras are used together to create activity in the centre corresponding to them. Once the activity has been created, the energy manifesting as a result of such activity can then be released through a further process of meditation.

Before going any further let us look at the chakras and their corresponding Yantras and Bija Mantras.

It is obviously a good idea to write the Bija Mantras down on separate cards, so that you become familiar with them. The Yantras are easy to make: paint them with the appropriate colours.

It is more beneficial to use, if possible, a translucent, brightly coloured paint, as this will facilitate the mental imagery process, thus aiding concentration.

CHAKRA	YANTRA	BIJA MANTRA
MULADHARA		'LAM'
SVADISTHANA		'VAM'
MANIPURA		'RAM'
ANAHATA		'YAM'
VISHUDDA		'HAM'
AJNA		'KSHAM'
SAHASRARA		'OM'

Exercise 33

Sit comfortably and relax. Chant the *Bija Mantras* in quick succession, beginning with 'Lam' and finishing with 'Om'.

Repeat the process three or four times, chanting through the seven *Bija Mantras*.

Now begin to clap your hands vigorously, in unison with each intonation. Continue for five minutes, longer if possible, then suspend the chanting and clapping, close your eyes and rest your hands on your solar plexus, feeling the vibration in your hands and through your entire body. In your imagination see the energy moving through the individual chakras, as though passing up from the earth, through the base chakra, working its way upwards, touching each chakra as it moves. When the vibration has ceased, resume the chanting for a further five minutes, then accompany it with clapping.

Repeat the process for twenty minutes; longer if you wish.

Once your eyes are closed see the energy moving through the chakras, taking to itself their inherent colours as it passes from one to the other. Allow the energy to move freely. If it appears, in your imagination, to be restricted in any way, mentally encourage it on its way.

This exercise is invigorating and has a tendency to stimulate the energy levels of the practitioner. Over a period of time it will heighten the awareness and make the psychic faculties much more responsive. It will also help to balance the individual chakras by creating in each the correct movement of energy.

 ## Exercise 34

With this exercise I would suggest that you work on one chakra a day, completing the entire system in one week. I would also suggest that it only be practised for one month out of three, so as to allow the results to take effect.

Place the first *Yantra* (yellow square) facing you at eye-level. Gaze at the centre of it without blinking. Stare until you can no longer look without blinking to clear your eyes. Close your eyes and place your hands over them. As soon as the after image of the *Yantra* appears in the mind's eye, introduce the corresponding *Bija Mantra* by inhaling a complete and full breath and sounding the word 'Lam' loudly and deeply on the exhalation. Close the lips at the end of the word and allow the 'M' sound to fill the air, until all the breath has been expelled.

Inhale a deep breath immediately, and repeat the chanting. Continue until the after image has dissolved completely.

Suspend the chanting. Open your eyes and return your gaze to the *Yantra*. Repeat the process.

Continue this exercise for ten minutes, longer if you feel comfortable with it.

Remember not to make the chanting laborious, as this will defeat the object of the exercise, which is of course to produce a calming, rhythmical effect upon the mind, and to introduce activity into the corresponding chakra.

In the Western world most people tend to be emotionally inhibited, and are very often enslaved by their emotions. But India, for example, does not appear to have the same problem, its people being very much in control of their insidious emotions. Meditation is often an integral part of the educational curriculum there, and today it is taught in many countries to very young children.

Children who have been taught meditation nearly always have less aggressive natures, and are often much more sensitive than those who have not learned it. This would substantiate the claims made by many notable meditation teachers that meditation alleviates stress and lessens the risk of heart disease.

However, there are many more benefits because, when practised regularly over a period of time, meditation can certainly heighten one's awareness and aid the cultivation of the creative and intuitive faculties.

Meditation enhances the quality of one's life and is capable of promoting longevity. In the 1960s, at the height of the so-called

'Flower Power' era, an Indian physicist, Maharishi Mahesh Yogi, was the innovator of a system of meditation which he called 'transcendental meditation'.

In this system a mantra was mentally repeated, without moving the lips or the tongue. Although the Maharishi claims that each mantra should be personal to the meditator, and that no mental force should be used, it is my belief that the word is of no great importance, and that almost any word may be used as long as the meditator feels comfortable with it.

Transcendental meditation is a modified version of some forms of yoga meditation in which the eyes should be closed and the attention turned inwards. When the mind wanders, the mantra should be reintroduced. It is extremely effective in controlling the mind and making it more focused. Incidentally, a cross-legged posture is not necessary when practising mantric meditation, unless you find it comfortable. Sitting on a straight-backed chair in the Egyptian posture will suffice – back straight, feet on the floor, head tilted slightly back. Unless you are a devotee of yoga, the lotus cross-legged position will be quite uncomfortable for you.

A mantra does not have to be a single word, it can be a whole phrase. One which I find most effective, both as a mantra and as a means of encouraging the development of the creative faculties, is the well-known 'Om mani padme hum', meaning 'Om, the jewel in the lotus'. This can be repeated mentally while visualizing a beautiful lotus flower containing within its petals a glistening, multi-faceted diamond, or some other precious gem. However, you will probably find this exercise quite difficult to achieve initially, so I would suggest using the mantra alone at first.

Although it is nearly always suggested that 'Om mani padme hum' be repeated mentally, I find that bringing it *audibly* to the lips helps to cultivate correct breath control, as well as producing some amazing vibrations in the surrounding air. Simply inhale a complete breath and commence chanting the sequence of words over and over again. I believe it is more effective if the phrase is chanted at least three times in succession before pausing for breath, but you must remember not to make it a labour. Should you feel it is simply not practical to audibly sound the mantra, repeat it mentally, not permitting any space to form between each word, so that one runs into the next. The lips and tongue should remain still, and the mind should be focused totally on the repetition of the phrase.

 ## Exercise 35

Focus your attention on the screen of your mind, and on it create a very still pond. See the light reflected across the surface of this pond, and even see your own reflection in the water. In the centre of the pond create a beautiful lotus flower, and see a small jewel in the centre of it. Make no attempt to mentally touch the jewel, but focus your attention on it totally. Be conscious of your breathing – keep it slow and even.

Determine all you can about the jewel in the lotus flower, mentally exploring its hidden qualities. Examine its perfume and the texture of its petals. Touch the jewel mentally with your fingers and feel its coolness and smoothness. See how the sunlight catches each facet, breaking up into numerous colours. Hold the picture of the jewel and the lotus flower steadily in the mind and absorb the stillness, the peace, the total serenity.

Once you have a clear picture fully established in your imagination, it may be a good idea to try and introduce the mantra 'Om mani padme hum'. Repeat it over and over again while you hold the picture steady in your mind.

As with other techniques, this exercise may be modified and changed in any way which suits your ability to focus and concentrate.

The mantra and the visualization can be used independently of each other; either way, the lotus flower exercise serves as a useful method of developing one's sensitivity and awareness.

It is easy to be put off by complex terminology and systems of meditation, but many people find that the most simplistic methods are the most effective.

It is important to experiment with as many techniques as possible until you find the method which suits you, and which is compatible with your capabilities.

Meditation is often productive of symbols, which can themselves be used as focal points for meditation. The following experiment in creative visualization is one such method, and one which most people enjoy and find quite easy to follow.

 Exercise 36

Imagine yourself standing on the bank of a very large lake. The water is clear and still in front of you. On the other side of the lake there are some mountains. The sky is very blue and clear, and the sun is shining full and bright and is reflected across the surface of the lake.

As you stand at the edge of the lake, feel the gentle breeze against your face. Listen to the birds whistling and singing unseen from the trees around you. Hear the monotonous drone of a bumble bee as it settles on a flower beside you. Drink in the peace and serenity of the scene around you.

As you gaze thoughtfully out across the lake, you notice a staircase emerging from the water, extending far up into the blueness above. Allow your attention to focus on the staircase. Feel yourself moving across the surface of the lake, without touching the water, until you come to rest at the foot of the staircase. Begin to climb the stairs, one step at a time. As you ascend, see the water below you still and calm. Move your eyes to the hills and mountains on the other side of the lake, and to the blue sky and the warm sun. Feel yourself passing through the blue of the sky until you are surrounded by it completely.

Reach the top of the staircase and pause for a moment to look around you. Feel yourself bathed in cool and relaxing vibrations of blue. As you glance to the side you notice a small casket appear, as if by magic. Mentally will the casket to move towards you. Pick it up. Hold it close and pull back the lid. Retrieve whatever is inside – let this be the first thing that comes into your mind. Do not change it, even if you find the object unpleasant.

You notice a piece of parchment and a pen also in the casket. Write a single word on the parchment and replace it in the casket, along with the pen and your object. Close the lid. Watch the casket move away from you, eventually disappearing into nothingness.

Begin your descent of the staircase, allowing your eyes to move about you all the time, watching the blue of the sky above you, and the lake below you moving nearer and nearer. See the hills and mountains, the sky and the bright sun.

Reach the foot of the stairs and feel yourself gliding across the surface of the water, until you finally settle once again on the grassy bank. Stand for a moment enjoying the peace and stillness; the birds singing in the trees, the gentle and hypnotic rustling of the leaves.

Allow your attention to move to the centre of the lake and see the staircase disappearing into the still water. Once it has gone completely, leaving slight ripples on the surface of the lake, breathe in slowly and deeply, and when you breathe out allow the picture to dissolve completely from your mind. Relax.

In this exercise you projected your consciousness into the meditation in which you experienced colour, sound and image.

Your ascent of the staircase symbolized the raising of the level of your awareness. At the top of the staircase you allowed yourself to interact with the blue of the sky and the casket.

Whatever you retrieved from the casket more than likely possessed symbolic meaning, and represented something of deep, spiritual significance. As the object was produced by your own subconscious, only *you* possess the power to interpret its true meaning. Take your object with you into future meditations and use it as a focal point.

While in the quietness, contemplate upon whatever you wrote on the piece of parchment. The next time you ascend the stairs in your meditation see if the word you wrote has changed.

Meditation is the means which all great minds have used to attain higher states of consciousness. However, the method is not so important, as long as the technique works for you and produces positive results.

Meditation is best practised at a time of day when you are not tired and likely to fall asleep. It should also be practised on an empty stomach, either before you have eaten or at least one hour after.

I always find it of great benefit to use the same room each time I meditate. If possible, create a small sanctuary for yourself. Burning some pleasant incense also helps to create the correct atmospheric conditions.

Dedication is vitally important where meditation is concerned. Try to practise your meditation consistently, at more or less the same time every day.

Never force meditation, and always look upon it as one endless experiment. Should you ever have a sense of having achieved something in meditation, then more than likely you have achieved nothing.

Try not to approach your meditation with any one particular aim in mind, for the achievement is in the actual practise of it. Therefore, although it is the object of this book to aid you in the development of your psychic powers, do not practise meditation with this specifically in mind. Make meditation an integral part of your daily routine – expect nothing, and you should achieve everything.

INDEX